ADVANCE PRAISE

"The number-one life skill that's not taught in schools is how to confidently and effectively handle money. I had to learn this the hard way, and when my kids got to the age where I had to start teaching them money skills, I was honestly kind of lost. That's when I found Chad and this book. If you want to save your kids the pain and heartache of learning about how to handle money, this is the book."

—TUCKER MAX, FOUR-TIME *NYT* BESTSELLING AUTHOR (SOLD OVER FIVE MILLION BOOKS) AND CO-FOUNDER OF SCRIBE

"I have six kids, three of whom we adopted from the foster system. Our adopted kids came from extreme poverty and now live in material abundance, which is new for both them and me. This book is an invaluable guide in helping me utilize my new and growing wealth to bless my children, not curse them."

—DR. BENJAMIN HARDY, ORGANIZATIONAL PSYCHOLOGIST AND AUTHOR OF *WHO NOT HOW* AND *THE GAP AND THE GAIN*

SMART, NOT SPOILED

SMART, NOT SPOILED

The 7 Money Skills Kids Must Master
Before Leaving the Nest

CHAD WILLARDSON, CRPC®, AWMA®

LIONCREST

PUBLISHING

SMART, NOT SPOILED

The 7 Money Skills Kids Must Master Before Leaving the Nest

ISBN   978-1-5445-2426-9 *Hardcover*

978-1-5445-2425-2 *Paperback*

978-1-5445-2424-5 *Ebook*

978-1-5445-2427-6 *Audiobook*

*This book is dedicated to my five children: McKinley,
Pierce, Sterling, Bentley, and Beckham.*

*Kids: Mom and I love you more than you could imagine! You are
growing up so quickly. I wish I could freeze time right now. My greatest
desire is to help you become successful and happy in whatever you
choose to pursue in your life. You are blessed with opportunities
and experiences that Mom and I never dreamed of while growing
up. We are not perfect parents, but we want what is best for you and
are doing all we can to teach you. It's not an easy thing to balance
prosperity with humility. But it's not impossible either. We strive to
make sure you learn to work hard, to struggle and stretch, and grow
your confidence while making decisions. Money is only a means to
an end. Money does not make you who you are, but it amplifies who
you are. People are more important than money. Always strive to do
good and be good with the opportunities and abundance that comes
your way. Reach for your dreams. Anything is possible with hard
work and faith in God. When it comes to money and life experiences,
be smart, not spoiled. As I've always told you, BE YOUR BEST.*

Love, Dad

CONTENTS

This book is not intended as a substitute for personalized financial guidance you may receive from your fiduciary advisor, attorney, or tax professional. The examples in this book are shared for educational purposes only. In many cases, identifying details have been removed.

INTRODUCTION

Kids these days have more—and expect more—than ever before. With the internet, social media, and technology in general, the push for having and doing everything is unprecedented. If you're like me, that's not at all how you grew up. And if you're like me, you want your kids to be smart, not spoiled.

Most of today's youth don't seem to appreciate the value of a dollar. But can we blame them? Is it even their fault? Have they really been taught anything about money?

More than likely, no. But the good news? That's what we're here to fix.

This topic is very important to me, professionally and personally. One of the reasons is that my family didn't have a lot of money growing up. I was taught to work hard and appreciate what we *did* have. We were a middle-income household, rarely even spending the money to go out to eat at restaurants. My parents shared a ten-year old used car. Though we didn't talk about money in our home, I'm grateful that I was raised in a humble environment where we learned to appreciate even the smallest things in life, like the ice cream truck that would drive by our neighborhood home once a week. The house I grew up in during my elementary years was just over 1,000 square feet in a very modest neighborhood of Southern California, but it's a very different situation for my kids today. They are growing up in abundance and prosperity, and that worries me a lot.

Maybe you've had those same feelings before. Doesn't it seem like kids today have so much compared to when we were younger? We have the challenge of raising our kids not to be entitled and to understand what it means to work. My desire to instill in them the important lessons from my own childhood drove my decision, for example, not to give them a weekly allowance— something I'll share more about in Chapter 3.

My background gives me a unique and important perspective in sharing the advice in this book. I've lived with and without a lot of money, have professionally advised countless families on their money issues, and I practice what I preach with my own children.

Before we get to the advice, let's take a closer look at why it's so necessary today.

BREAKING THE CYCLE

"Have you ever gotten a bad grade on a test or in a class and been upset about it?"

I've asked this question to start my presentation dozens of times to thousands of students at school assemblies.

Each time, their hands shoot up in the air.

Then, I show them the first slide of my presentation, which is a big, fat, red letter F.

"This is the grade I give our education system," I say.

They gasp. Eyes get wide. And then they cheer. Every single time.

They're so excited to give that grade back for once. And though I might get some sideways glances from the teachers and administrators in the room, I know I've gotten the kids' attention at that point. This opens the floor for me to explain that I'm giving out this F grade because schools are failing to teach kids about personal finance.

Most teens graduate high school knowing how to dissect a frog and can name the inner parts of a cell but don't know how to set a personal budget, invest for retirement, borrow money, pay taxes, or any of the other financial basics that affect every single adult's life.

This isn't a problem of the past. Even today, my own five kids aren't learning about this in their classes at school.

As adults, we often take for granted the basic concepts of personal finance. Or worse yet, we don't even understand them ourselves. I'd categorize the seven main areas of personal finance to include the following: investing, loans and borrowing, budgeting and financial planning, earning income, taxes, insurance, and giving. Our kids aren't getting this financial foundation anywhere, so it's up to us to teach them.

Why? Because raising children to be self-confident and financially independent as they begin life as young adults is very important for their future success. Children develop their feelings and attitudes about money at a very young age, and this early blueprint will stick with them their entire life. Through thoughtful financial education, you have the opportunity to shape your child's future as a contributing member of society—someone who doesn't just work to pay bills but who actually creates some abundance and makes the world a better place.

I know what you're thinking: "OK, great. I'm in! But how do I talk to my kids about all these things? Where do I start? What do I even say?" A recent study reports that although 75 percent of parents think that providing financial guidance for their kids is part of their duty as parents, only 36 percent report having any clarity on how to do that.

Let's begin to answer that question by looking at the past: How did *your* parents talk to *you* about money? What was the attitude around money discussions in *your* home? Did they even talk about it with you? Or were you left trying to figure these things out on your own? The hard way. The stressful way. The way we don't want for our kids.

If you know me or if you read my last book, you know I don't believe money has to be a stressful part of your life. That's why I'm here to help you break that cycle.

And it *is* a cycle. Take a moment to think of the generations before you and after you. This is your moment to shape the way your family and future generations approach the topic of money. If you've come from a dysfunctional place, you have the chance to completely change course starting today.

Many people only talk about money when they're arguing and upset. As a result, kids see money as a negative topic and the source of family contention. It scares them and causes stress, which also takes a toll on their mental and physical health. How could we then expect them to feel comfortable talking to their parents or future spouses about money?

Young people report it's easier for parents to discuss drugs and sex with them than to discuss money—which is to say that these conversations rarely happen. Money's taboo status leads people to repeat financial mistakes. Breaking that cycle in your family requires facing the facts. Money causes problems when we don't know enough about it and don't feel like we can talk about it. It becomes shrouded in danger and mystery.

Most of us developed our attitude towards money based on lessons our parents taught us (or didn't teach us), often indirectly. The influence of your beliefs and values and how you treat money will forever impact your family members. My goal is to help you raise financially thoughtful kids and make money a comfortable topic of conversation in your family. It doesn't have to be so intimidating. This book will empower you with ideas, tools, and resources to teach your kids how to be successful, confident, and financially fluent, well-prepared for their future.

You're not alone in this dilemma. While my parents are wonderful people and taught me and my younger sisters a great deal about integrity, hard work, and service, I can't say they taught me much about personal finance. They definitely encouraged us to prioritize giving and saving and to be thoughtful with our money. I do remember my mom always recording transactions in her checkbook ledger, and that she used coupons frequently at the grocery store. I personally had a job from the age of fifteen and knew it was important to work hard and to save money, but I didn't actually understand personal finance at all.

I didn't know what I didn't know because my family didn't have an ongoing discussion about money at home. In fact, for the most part, it felt like a touchy subject. And, of course, I didn't learn about it in school, either. Once I entered my profession as a financial advisor, I felt inspired to teach people they don't have to be scared or intimidated about the financial world and money conversations with their family.

I understand why so many avoid it, though. Money is a sensitive subject. You may feel like it's too private or confidential or be overwhelmed with the anxiety of it all. Money mistakes have long-term consequences. You can't bring your best self to your family and to the world if your personal financial life is a mess. Being financially stable allows you to make a meaningful impact everywhere you go. Without that anchor of financial stability, your boat will capsize. It's hard to help yourself, let alone others, in that situation. There's a lot to lose when it comes to money.

We don't want that situation for you, for your kids, or for your grandkids.

The cycle ends now, on your watch. You can break free from all the old patterns and habits, the negative stigma, the arguments, and whatever other financial baggage you inherited from your parents, grandparents, or other influences in your young life. You can flip the script with your kids and make a lasting impact for their future. You can help them have a confident, healthy relationship with money.

The good news is that it doesn't have to be hard! Besides being simple, many of the tips and activities I will share with you in this book are even fun for both you and your children.

> My goal is to help you raise financially thoughtful kids and make money a comfortable topic of conversation in your family.

WHY THESE SEVEN MONEY SKILLS?

If you teach your kids how to **invest early and often**, they'll be on track for financial freedom and independence. They'll make smart choices with their money and know how to take advantage of opportunities. They won't just follow the crowd and make the same mistakes everyone else does. If they understand investing and compound interest at an early age, they'll end up with many times more wealth than they would otherwise. They'll have more opportunities to increase their own passive income. Financial security will show up in their life much sooner and they'll avoid being scammed or falling for get-rich-quick schemes.

If your child understands how to **borrow wisely**, they'll understand the difference between good and bad debt. They'll use borrowing strategically and intentionally to enhance their life and won't risk financial ruin by overborrowing. They'll know the difference between "good debt" and "bad debt." They'll be more confident about when and how to borrow and from whom. If they understand how lending works, they'll be better prepared to interact with banks and lenders, which they'll have to deal with their whole life. They won't fall for the traps of expensive or dangerous loans.

If kids **know their cash flow**, they won't get stuck in the rat race, living paycheck to paycheck for fifty years. They'll understand what they can afford and make the most of buying and investing opportunities. They'll experience less stress and more control over their money. They won't have to worry about unexpected expenses derailing their family life because they will be prepared. A budget is a savvy way of intentionally controlling your money, so money does not control you. It allows you to know where your money's coming from, where you're spending it, and how much you'll have at the end of the month, giving you a complete understanding of your finances. Kids who know how to track income and expenses will be more organized and won't feel afraid to talk about money in their own families when they grow up. They'll be smarter consumers.

If kids are comfortable **talking taxes**, they'll understand the true cost of everything they earn and buy. They'll make better investment decisions with regard to stocks, real estate, and businesses. They won't get blindsided by unexpected tax bills. They'll be better prepared in their financial planning and better informed of the rules and their rights. They'll have more peace of mind come tax time instead of feeling stressed out.

If kids have a grasp on **learning to earn**, they'll be more creative in looking for opportunities to make money. They'll be better at negotiating job offers, starting businesses, and more prepared choosing their future career. They'll understand how the world works, how to earn a specific amount of money to sustain the lifestyle they want, and what the true definition of success and wealth looks like for them (spoiler alert: it's not all about the dollars and cents).

If kids understand insurance as a way to **protect who and what they care about**, they won't be caught off guard when emergencies arise. I have so many unfortunate stories of people facing unnecessary hardship because they weren't prepared. Insurance protects your family and your business against catastrophes. Kids who learn about insurance will be better prepared and have more peace of mind and confidence for the future. They'll behave more responsibly, because they'll understand claims and accidents are expensive. They'll also feel safer.

Kids who **give generously** will have a healthier relationship with money. They'll be less selfish and understand money is simply a tool that can be used. They'll be better global citizens and have a heart for those in need. They'll also find more fulfillment and joy in their own success, if they learn to be good at giving.

HOW DO I USE THIS BOOK?

This book is designed as a resource to help you raise financially thoughtful kids who are smart, not spoiled. Each chapter shares the key insights of one financial topic. My goal is that you find the information to be easy to understand and share with the young people in your life. I intentionally have not included everything there is to know about these financial concepts for a couple reasons: First, that's not possible in one book. Second, I want your kids to be able to focus on and master the most important skills and principles from each category.

As I explain each of these seven core principles of personal finance, I will share stories and actual things my wife and I have done with our five children. Additionally, I've gathered some great stories and sample activities used by my friends and clients that I am excited to share with you. I'm grateful for their contributions and happy to report that, even while I was writing this book, I learned some new, fun things to try with *my* own family. It's been a win–win.

It's time to remove the fear and avoidance around talking about personal finance and equip your kids to knock it out of the park when they head out into the world on their own. This goes for boys and girls alike. In fact, it's especially important to teach your girls about money and business and to break the cycle of putting limited expectations or ceilings on what they're exposed to. Don't shortchange the young girls in your family. I talk to my daughters about money and business just as much as, if not more than, I do with my sons. The bottom line? Girls or boys, you can empower your children to eventually launch independently, confidently—and ultimately, smart, not spoiled.

Let's get started.

CHAPTER 1

INVEST EARLY
AND OFTEN

"Investing is laying out money now to get more money back in the future."

—WARREN BUFFETT

"Would you rather receive $100,000 every day for one month or a penny today that doubles in value every day for one month?"

This is what I heard, sitting at a hotel restaurant in St. Thomas last year—from a ten-year-old kid. I watched him hit his dad's arm and excitedly ask the question again, waiting for an answer.

His dad said, "One hundred thousand every day, buddy—that's $3 million, easy money!"

The kid replied, "Wrong, Dad! That's not the right answer! You could've had over $5 million if you chose the penny option instead."

(At this point, I thought I'd better make this kid a job offer.)

"That's impossible," said the dad.

"No, it's not! Look: I will show you how much the penny grows to," the kid said. Then, he literally pulled up the calculator app on his dad's phone, did the math, and showed his dad the effects of compound growth. So impressive!

"Let me see that," said the dad, taking his phone back. He was stunned, and so was I—both by the genius of this young kid and by the dad's shortsighted reply.

THE POWER
OF COMPOUNDING

> If you were to double $0.01 every day
> for 30 days, you would have...

Day 1	$0.01	Day 11	$10.24	Day 21	$10,485.76
Day 2	$0.02	Day 12	$20.48	Day 22	$20,971.52
Day 3	$0.04	Day 13	$40.96	Day 23	$41,943.04
Day 4	$0.08	Day 14	$81.92	Day 24	$83,886.08
Day 5	$0.16	Day 15	$163.84	Day 25	$167,772.16
Day 6	$0.32	Day 16	$327.68	Day 26	$335,554.32
Day 7	$0.64	Day 17	$655.36	Day 27	$671,088.64
Day 8	$1.28	Day 18	$1,310.72	Day 28	$1,342,177.28
Day 9	$2.56	Day 19	$2,621.44	Day 29	$2,684,353.56
Day 10	$5.12	Day 20	$5,242.88	Day 30	$5,368,709.12

Kids actually love to talk about money and share what they've learned. This budding investor's financial riddle demonstrates a key lesson for everyone, particularly young people: **invest as much as you can as early as you can**, and you will reap the benefits in the future.

If you don't think about the power of compound interest, you wouldn't assume a penny would grow to $5 million in one month. Of course, that doubling every day for thirty days represents an impossible interest rate in the real world, but that's not the point. The exercise simply teaches the principle and the power of compound growth.

The kid's excitement reminded me of my own "aha" moment growing up. When I was a sophomore in high school, one of my teachers went off topic and gave our class a short lesson on compound interest that I will never forget. He said if we saved one hundred dollars a month from age fifteen until age sixty-five and invested it at a rate of 10 percent growth per year, it would turn into $1,762,188.

The number blew my mind. How was that growth even possible? Without interest, one hundred dollars a month for fifty years only totals $60,000. How could investing $60,000 add an extra $1.7 million just from growth? The answer is through the magic of compound interest! A light bulb turned on in my head, and I couldn't stop thinking about the lesson all month.

Years later I ended up getting my bachelor's degree in economics and finding my way to this industry and career of helping people strive for personal financial freedom. It's all I've ever done since college, and I love it! This is a great reminder that what you teach your kids now might spark a lifelong interest. (And worst case, it prepares them for a better future. Another win–win.)

WHAT DO I TEACH MY KIDS ABOUT MONEY NOW VS. MONEY LATER?

When you receive money from any source, you have only two choices: use it today, or use it in the future. The four primary uses of money include: spend it, give it, save it, or invest it. This is simple enough for even your younger kids to understand.

The pro of spending your money right now is you get what you need immediately, but the con is you won't have that money to spend later and won't benefit from potential interest earnings or growth. Many kids (and adults) love the thrill of spending money right after receiving it.

Giving money away also means you won't have it later, but it has the benefit of helping charities and people in need, bringing joy to both the giver and the receiver.

Saving means setting money aside for the short-term in an account that keeps your money available at all times. The safety feature is a pro, but the con is that your money won't earn much interest and doesn't grow.

Choosing to invest carries more risk because investments can lose value. However, if you choose investments that gain value in the long term, then you can grow your money significantly higher than you put in.

Investing is simply delayed spending. I tell my kids if they choose not to spend money or give it away today, then they're choosing to use it in the future, which gives it a chance to grow so they could have more to spend or give anyway.

> *"Building wealth is a marathon, not a sprint. The keys to success include consistency, patience, and discipline."*
>
> —UNKNOWN

WHAT DO I TEACH MY KIDS ABOUT SAVING VS. INVESTING?

People regularly ask me what they should invest their money

in. When it comes to saving versus investing, my personal philosophy is based on your time frame of when you will need the money back. If you plan to spend the money in under five years, you should save rather than invest. If your need for spending your money is beyond five years, then investing is often a better choice because of the potential growth. Of course, there are exceptions, but this is a good guideline to teach your kids.

> **PARENT TIP**
>
> Should I invest for my child's future college expenses? I get this question a lot too, and the answer is...it depends, again, on time between now and when you will need the money. If we're talking about a junior or senior in high school, I don't think the risk of investing is generally worth it. At this point, college is only a couple of years off. There's no reliable way to predict whether the markets will go up or down between your child's sophomore and senior year. On the other hand, if your child is ten or better yet, three years old, then yes, absolutely invest! You've got eight to fifteen years, and I can more confidently say the money invested will be worth more with that amount of time.

Let's break this principle down with an example you can use to explain it to your kids. If someone wants to buy a house in three years and has saved up for their down payment, then I don't recommend they invest the money needed for that big purchase. I know everyone wants a quick investment return and more money for the down payment, but it's better to be safe and smart about it than to risk losing it. Put that cash in a savings account. Of course, in those two years, the investment *could've* increased—but the opposite could've also happened. If there

were a big drop in the markets, they'd find themselves with less purchasing power right when they needed it most.

The bottom line? You can't afford a decrease if you need to make a big preplanned purchase and have just enough money for it—whether a house, a car, or college tuition—at a specific point in time. On the other hand, when your spending needs are further into the future, you can more easily weather the storms and cycles of the markets and enjoy much greater growth in the meantime.

Investing takes strategy and patience. It's not a quick fix or an easy way to make a buck. (Obviously, we're not talking about day trading or cryptocurrencies here. That's a whole other gamble for a whole other book.) There are many ways to lose money quickly when "investing" it. Teach your kids to avoid get-rich-quick schemes. Typically, if an opportunity sounds way too good to be true, it probably is.

WHAT DO I TEACH MY KIDS ABOUT INVESTMENT CATEGORIES?

There are four primary categories I see people investing in: stocks, bonds, real estate, and private businesses. This list of four is certainly not all-inclusive, but the hundreds of trillions invested in these categories along with the many years of historical data available make them important enough to touch on in this chapter.

THE STOCK MARKET

"The stock market" refers to the collection of publicly traded companies all around the world. Stock market investing is a core financial topic to teach young people. Kids should also understand the common ways in which you can invest in the stock market, namely owning stocks, mutual funds, and ETFs.

"I talk to my kids (ages thirteen and nine) about money regularly and have been talking to them since they were about five. Every chance I get I drive home to them the importance of saving and investing for retirement. I told them I wasn't taught this and learned the hard way. To this day, we'll get in the car, and I'll say, 'I want to talk to you about something.' They'll immediately groan in unison, 'Dad, you aren't going to talk to us about investing and retirement again, are you?'

"One day, I took out a stock calculator and said to them, 'Kids, if your mother and I had invested in Apple when we first got married, starting with $1,000 and investing only $100 a month, today it would be worth almost $4 million.' I swear both of them said the same thing at the same time: 'It would be worth how much? Why didn't you do that?'

"It was funny, but it really taught them why it's important to invest early and often."

—TOM SILVER, SENIOR MANAGER, SPARTAN FINANCIAL SERVICES

STOCKS

Stocks represent direct ownership in large, publicly owned companies. Examples include Tesla, Facebook, Google, Nike, Amazon, Costco, Apple, Disney, Coca-Cola, McDonald's, and Netflix. When talking to your kids about stocks, I recommend naming companies they're familiar with because they use their products and services. They might be fascinated to learn that even as kids, they can actually be "part owners" in those companies.

Kids might not understand all the ins and outs of stocks, but they'll grasp that people can put their money into big companies. When a company makes more money, grows, sells more products, and is successful, then the money you invest in it goes up in value. You want to invest in companies you believe will continue to do well in the future.

There's really no amount too little to invest. Each stock has a different price per share, but they all offer a potential return on investment. The share price of a stock is less important than the growth rate (percentage return) of the price of the stock.

For example, Amazon's stock share price is quite high—over $3,000 at the time of this writing. Most young people starting out will not have enough to even buy one share of Amazon. Netflix stock, on the other hand, is less than $500 a share. Nike and Beyond Meat are in the low one hundreds. There's a huge range in prices per share across the global stock market.

New and young investors make the mistake of thinking those price differences matter and that this means one company is more valuable than another simply because of the share price. They might assume that means it must be a better investment because the price per share is higher. That's false. You can't learn about the fundamental strength and prospects of a company based solely on how expensive the stock shares are. And the potential growth of your invested money is also not dependent on the price per share. For example, if you buy a stock for ten dollars and it goes to twenty dollars, you just doubled your investment. It doesn't matter if it starts out as ten dollars a share or $5,000 a share. As an investor, all that matters to you is the percentage by which it rises or falls.

Initial price per share isn't the important consideration for you. What really matters is the percentage change after you invest, because that number represents what return you get as an investor.

You can explain this to your kids with this simple example: if you buy one share of a stock that cost $3,000 and it went up in price to $3,300, it's the same as you investing to own 300 shares of a ten-dollar stock that only goes up by just one dollar per share after you invested. The result will be the exact same. A 10 percent increase on your original investment of $3,000.

If your kids are old enough to take the conversation one step further, explore this with them: if you buy a stock at twenty dollars that goes to twenty-two dollars, which could happen in one day, you've achieved 10 percent growth. By contrast, if you put your money in a bank account earning 0.1 percent (which is actually higher than current interest rates at the banks), it would take you sixty or seventy years to get the same growth, assuming interest rates stayed like this.

MUTUAL FUNDS

A mutual fund is a professionally managed investment fund made up of a pool of money collected from many investors. Mutual funds invest in stocks, bonds, and other investments, but investors don't directly own those particular investments. Instead, they own shares of the fund. It's like having twenty kids around a table, and they each put down three dollars, making a pool of sixty dollars total. Then, they invest that money as a group in different companies.

The mutual fund pools together money with other people to own investments, but each investor actually only owns a piece of the group bucket of money. If you buy shares in a mutual fund, you don't own the Apple or Facebook stock directly. Instead, as a member of the fund group, you get proportional gains when the fund's investments go up or down.

A mutual fund gives small individual investors access to diversified, professionally managed portfolios. If you don't have enough money to buy a diverse range of individual stocks, you can instead buy shares of a mutual fund that owns 500 or 1,000 companies. Doing so allows you to diversify and spread out your money, even if you're a smaller or newer investor. Most retirement plans invest in mutual funds.

ETFS

ETF stands for "exchange-traded fund." An ETF is a hybrid of a stock and a mutual fund. It's a basket of investments that tracks a market index or industry category. ETFs are similar to mutual funds, except they can be bought and sold throughout the day, just like stocks. If you were confident technology would continue to grow through the pandemic with people at home, then it would make sense for you to invest funds in a technology ETF tracking that sector. If many technology companies in the fund did well, grew, and made more profits, then that ETF would go up in value—and you'd benefit. PS: that's exactly what just happened.

There are thousands of types of ETFs, some of which track the entire stock market, real estate markets, bond markets, etc. The benefit of ETFs is they're typically less expensive and easier to buy and sell than mutual funds. ETFs are in between the two: they still get diversification by tracking many different companies, but they don't have the high fees of so many mutual funds. They also don't have the high risk of just owning a few individual stocks by themselves.

BONDS

Bonds essentially make you a lender. A bond could be thought of as an IOU between you (the lender) and the borrower that includes the details of the loan and its payments. Bonds are used by companies and governments to fund their projects and operations. As a bond investor, you *lend* money to companies or governments instead of investing for *ownership*. Young people shouldn't really be buying in bonds because they're super conservative investments with lower potential returns. When you lend money, you typically get a fixed return based on the interest agreement, just like when a bank lends you money to buy a house or to go to school at a fixed rate. Like stocks, you can invest in bonds individually and directly, through mutual funds, and through ETFs.

When you buy stocks, stock mutual funds, and stock ETFs, you own parts of companies. When the companies inside those investments increase earnings and become more valuable, you get significantly more growth on your money. Young people have so much time for growth that they'll make far more money by being owners rather than lenders. When you have bonds in your account over a long period of time, the returns are lower than the stock market. Bond investments would be more appropriate for older investors but aren't typically recommended for kids. Bonds tend to be safer than stocks, but there's a big price (opportunity cost and also inflation) to pay for that safety.

REAL ESTATE

Real estate categories include residential, commercial, and multifamily investments. It's important for kids to understand there are owners of every piece of property they see whether it's land, houses, apartments, hotels, or businesses. Owning real estate is one of the major financial commitments that American families make in their lifetimes.

My kids were fascinated when they started understanding a little bit more about real estate. If we went to a local hamburger place, I'd explain the hamburger restaurant might rent its building and parking lot from an investor or the person who owns the restaurant might also own the land and the building. When they go to the doctor's office, either the doctor owns the building or someone else owns it and the doctor pays rent to run their medical business there. When they see an apartment complex, someone owns those apartments, is in charge of managing the property for the tenants, and earns income from the rents paid each month.

Kids also tend to be fascinated by Zillow. My kids love using Zillow on our family ipad to hover over a neighborhood on the satellite view, looking at different houses, and clicking to see the estimated value. Zillow's estimates aren't perfect, but the site still offers an interesting, easy way to teach children about real estate. When we go on our family bike rides in Balboa (Newport Beach, California), they love to see the different beautiful beach houses and guess how much they might cost. They've learned that houses on bigger lots with more bedrooms cost more. Houses in popular areas, such as neighborhoods close to Disneyland or the beach, cost more. Those in less desirable areas cost less. As kids explore, they start to see the patterns in real estate value and pay attention to which houses sell for how much.

My kids also know our family's personal real estate story. I bought my first home in 2005 and as a wealth advisor at Merrill Lynch with a few years under my belt. My wife and I had a seven-month-old baby and were ages twenty-three and twenty-six. The housing market was extremely expensive—actually overpriced—at the time. It was not a great time to be buying a first house, and it was a stretch just to purchase a modest single-story. However, we didn't want to wait for a "buyer's market," because we'd outgrown our small condo and wanted to become home-owners. We wanted to start building equity.

This home would be our starter home for our small family, but we knew it would not be the last home we'd ever move into. Because of that, we did not invest too much money into that first house and did our own paint job and laid tile down ourselves. Instead of putting too much more money into that home, we saved monthly for a future deposit for our next house we'd someday move into. A few years after living there, the Great Recession hit. Prices of homes dropped more than 50 percent. In late 2009, we were able to buy the house of our dreams in a significantly discounted short sale. A short sale occurs when the bank is about to foreclose on a house because the owner hasn't been paying their mortgage, but it agrees to resell the property for less than the value of the mortgage. In our case, the sellers owed the bank $1.9 million on their mortgage, but we bought the house for only $850,000.

In the middle of the craziness of the recession, the bank was happy to get rid of it and not have the hassle of owning it any-more. I believe teaching your kids about what happened in real estate (and the stock market) during the Great Recession of 2007–2009 is a great way to discuss how markets fluctuate. Ideally, with any investment, you want to buy at a discount and sell at a profit—and we certainly succeeded with getting our house at a discount. If there were only four words your kids could take away regarding investing, they'd be "**buy low, sell high.**"

Now, our original house is turned into a cash-flowing rental property. From 2009 to 2012, we continued to buy dozens of rental properties, both single- and multifamily. When the real estate investments became too big for us to manage on our own, we hired a full-time property management company. I've taught my kids about how property management works. We visit some of the properties and look at them together, and I'll talk to them about some issues we're having with maintenance and repairs. We recently had to replace a roof and fix a water leak, and it cost a full month's rent on this particular property. We discuss challenges and opportunities of real estate with our kids, to give them some insight into the investment process. Because we show both sides of the equation, the positives and the negatives, they understand owning rentals isn't as simple as purchasing a property and collecting rent in perpetuity, hassle-free.

> "All of our talks with our young kids revolve around real estate invest-ing because that's what we know best. Their goal is to have their first rental property by age sixteen (with our help, of course), but they are earning their own money and saving for the down payment. Then, they will want to buy a property every six months after that first investment. That's our hope."
>
> —JONNY AND SUZETTE BAIRD, REAL ESTATE INVESTORS
> AND LUXURY VRBO PROPERTY OWNERS

PRIVATE BUSINESSES

I've taught my children the difference between starting a business, being a partner in a business, and investing in a company, and I have experience doing all three.

I started Pacific Capital in 2011, which took not only financial commitment but also countless hours of work and what's often called "sweat equity"—building the business from scratch. I'm a co-founder and co-owner of the Draft Sports Complex in Southern California; multiple co-founders and co-owners put money into the venture to start it and keep it going. We work together as a team to grow the business and had to deal with many challenges during the pandemic recently. I've also invested in many private businesses, some which have worked out to be successful and some of which haven't.

One of the biggest differences among those three types of business investments is in the third one: simply investing money in a business, you likely don't have much or any control over the day-to-day decisions. You hope the business leadership team makes good choices, but you invest in the business based on trust in them without having direct influence yourself.

By contrast, partners in a private business may have some influence, but they have to reconcile their different goals, wishes, and priorities of multiple people with different backgrounds, areas of expertise, and financial situations. Partners often have challenges when one wants a certain level of income to withdraw from the business, but another wants to leave the money in the business and expand. There are many possible competing visions for a given business. At the same time, you have the benefit of other people to bounce ideas off of and help solve problems. Partnerships also offer more financial resources to share in the burden when expenses are high.

When you start a business on your own, you assume all the

risk yourself—all the financial commitments, decisions, and everything else are on your shoulders. My kids already have the experience of starting their own trash can collection business in our neighborhood. It started with one of the neighbors asking for help with taking out the trash and bringing in the bins when they were going to be gone for a two-week trip. The kids did it just as a favor, but when the neighbors got back, they insisted on giving my kids some money for their work. They wouldn't take no for an answer and asked what the kids thought was a fair price. They all agreed on a dollar per trash can.

The next week, one of the kids asked if the neighbors would like help with their trash again, just to earn some more money. Now, they have an ongoing small income stream. They're responsible for writing out and submitting their invoices and handling all aspects of the business. If they don't follow through, they don't get paid. Their neighborhood enterprise is nothing big and makes very little money for them, but it offers a valuable learning experience for them.

WHAT DO I TEACH MY KIDS ABOUT INFLATION?

One basic economic principle your kids need to understand is that of inflation. To teach my kids about inflation, I've shown them pictures of basic items they're familiar with, comparing the costs a long time ago to now. Visuals are important. Inflation isn't actually a hard concept for children to understand. Even our seven-year-old grasps the importance when I point out that a movie ticket costs twelve dollars, whereas it was two dollars when I was her age. She knows as she grows up, many things will cost more.

1970 cost:
$0.65

2021 cost:
$6.50

This fact that costs are rising reinforces why **it's important to invest early and often and benefit from compound interest**. Many people don't realize if you never invest because you're afraid of risk, then you're actually taking a much greater risk—by guaranteeing your money will lose value to inflation over time. Your money loses value as it sits idle in a bank account earning nothing (because that is exactly what interest rates are paying these days).

WHAT DO I TEACH MY KIDS ABOUT GOAL-DRIVEN INVESTING?

It's important not to be so risk-averse that you never invest, but it's also essential to realize all successful investing is goal-focused and planning-driven. When kids and young people start investing, they need to understand the importance of not simply gambling their money away. Investing requires strategy and patience.

PARENT TIP

This lesson is for kids, of course, but it's also one I've run across at times with adults. Remember that putting money in the stock market is more complex than buying a lotto ticket—or at least, it should be if you want to achieve long-term success. Too often even adults don't have a plan when they invest. They just give money to a financial advisor and hope it all works out. Or they get excited about a particular stock and buy it with nothing more than a strong hope that the investment will go up. Hope is great, but hope is not a strategy. If you don't know how to invest with a plan, consult a financial fiduciary to help you create one. You may also find some good insights on this topic in my first book, *Stress-Free Money*.

When talking about investing and goals, encourage your kids to consider the risks and benefits as well as creating a plan for any particular investment before proceeding. Ask: What are your long-term goals for your money? Why? What will you eventually use this money for? What are your expectations for the investment? Are these expectations realistic? When do you plan to sell the stock? How will you get your money back if you need it? How will you know whether or not your investment is a success?

Normalizing these conversations today will take the guesswork out of their investment activities in the future—or at least lay the groundwork of knowledge they need to make smart decisions with their money.

WHAT DO I TEACH MY KIDS ABOUT WHEN TO INVEST?

I didn't start investing right away after my light bulb moment in high school. Unfortunately, I was making minimum wage at a crappy job and didn't really pursue any side hustles to earn enough money to begin investing. However, that lesson about compound interest still planted a seed for me.

Today, I wish I'd invested just a little back in high school. For your kids, it is possible to invest a little bit every week, even if they have a low-paying job. It's particularly good to encourage them to invest in a Roth individual retirement account (Roth IRA). A contribution to a Roth IRA for Kids can be made if a minor has earned income during the year. Eligible income can include formal employment income or self-employment income. Activities like babysitting or mowing lawns can even qualify a minor for Roth IRA contributions. If they are earning money, then they can start reaping the benefits of compound interest very early on. This money then can grow for fifty years or more!

Why does this matter? Consider this example: **if you save $10,000 a year in your twenties and then stop on your thirtieth birthday, you'll have as much money as someone who starts at age thirty and continues all the way to age sixty.** Think about that. Saving and investing for ten years results in more wealth in the long run than someone saving and investing for thirty years, simply because the person investing for ten years gave themselves a head start and had more time for growth. The massive benefit comes not from earning and saving more money but from **starting earlier and having longer for the interest to compound.** You can invest much less money and still get the same results if you start earlier.

This analogy might help your kids really grasp what compound investing is: compound interest works like a snowball rolling downhill. The time invested equals how steep the slope is. The snowball equals your investment portfolio. The steeper the slope and the more powder you add to the snowball, the larger it will become.

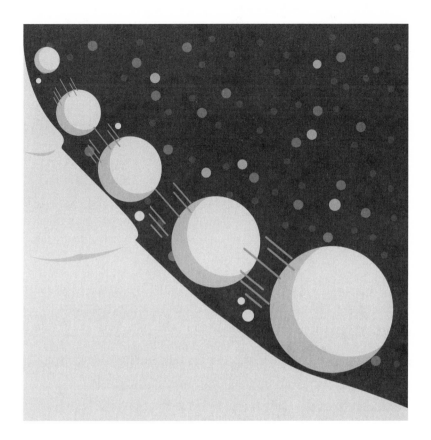

There's not a hard-and-fast rule about how much to invest, and every situation is different. The important thing is to teach your kids the importance of setting aside a small amount to save and invest early on (and regularly) so that it becomes a lifelong habit.

> *"We openly discussed the significant wealth our kids have a chance of inheriting. We had one large family meeting where we hypothetically gave each adult child $1 million to invest on January 1, promising to track it with them. It's a way for us to teach responsible investing without putting our money at risk. We are also starting a family book club with required monthly reading and will make sure to discuss many investing and personal finance topics with them as they are raising their young families!"*
>
> —CHARLES AND DIANE CHACON, REAL ESTATE INVESTORS, REALTORS

WHAT DO I TEACH MY KIDS ABOUT OTHER LONG-TERM INVESTMENT VEHICLES?

There are other specialized accounts that can help set kids up for financial success and leverage compound interest.

529 COLLEGE ACCOUNTS

This one is for you, Mom or Dad: 529 is the designation for a tax-advantaged college savings account in the US. Parents or guardians (or anyone feeling generous towards supporting your kids' future education) put money into it and invest in a mutual fund, similar to a 401(k). You don't have to pay taxes on the interest or the growth, as long as you eventually use it for approved, college-related expenses.

I didn't earn a high annual income when my first daughter was born in 2004, so I was only saving twenty-five dollars a month in her investment account at the time. But I still started investing for her when she was just one week old. I've gradually increased that monthly amount as my income has risen over the years. Now, she's sixteen, and more than 60 percent of the account's value represents the growth from compounding over her life, not the deposits I made. The younger you start investing, the more opportunity it has for the compound growth to outweigh the money you put in.

UTMA

UTMA stands for the Uniform Transfers to Minors Act, which allows minors to receive gifts and money in special accounts with a custodian. Guardians can open an investment account for their children to get them started. Grandparents and other adults can deposit money into the account as gifts, and children themselves can make deposits as well. It offers the minor account holder a chance to learn how to invest and manage money responsibly, under the supervision of a responsible adult.

DO TRY THIS AT HOME: LEARNING ACTIVITIES FOR THE FAMILY

When teaching your kids about money, I encourage you to include the whole family and make the lessons fun and engaging. Here are a few ideas for family activities.

CASHFLOW for Kids. This board game is similar to Monopoly...but so much better. It's so popular that it keeps selling out and experiencing price spikes. All my children enjoy it and ask to play over and over together. This game is a worthy investment, as it's the best board game I know of that teaches kids about investing and money. Players get to see the effect of borrowing to make purchases, increasing monthly expenses, and choosing assets to invest in based on how much they cost and how much passive income they will pay in the future. The goal is to invest in assets that generate more in passive income than the cost of your recurring expenses. The moment you hit that goal and "escape the rat race," you win the game. There are a lot of video and board games on the market these days. Why not harness your child's love of competition in a way that will teach them how to be financially successful? Playing as a family also gives you a chance to have great conversations about money and choices.

DIY Marshmallow Experiment. You've probably heard of the Marshmallow Experiment. In 1972, Stanford conducted a study led by psychologist Walter Mischel to examine delayed gratification. In the study, a child could choose between one small but immediate reward (a marshmallow or a pretzel stick, depending on the child's preference)—or two small rewards if they waited for a period of time. The researcher left the room for about fifteen minutes, during which time the children had the one tempting treat in front of them, and then returned. If they didn't eat the one, they received two as a reward. In follow-up studies, the researchers found that children who were able to wait longer for the preferred rewards tended to have better life outcomes, as measured by SAT scores, educational attainment, personal income, body mass index (BMI), and other life measures. Do your own marshmallow patience experiment with young children. Tell your child they can have a piece of candy at lunchtime. Or, if they wait until after dinner, they can receive two pieces of candy. The process teaches them patience can earn them a greater reward over time. Most kids will probably want the candy right away, but if you show them how much more they'll get if they wait a bit, this lesson will sink in. Typically, it takes years to see the average stock market return of almost 10 percent, which means investors need to take the long view about the market's ups and downs. Showing your kids how patience pays off offers a very valuable investing lesson for their future.

Bring Reality into the Conversation. For younger children, bring up companies that produce items they use. Physically have these items out. For example, have an iPad and talk about Apple, or watch the newest movie together and talk about Disney. Explain that these big companies are looking for people to be "part owners" by investing in stocks. As they get older, have a mock investment and allow them to track stocks for six months. Encourage them to learn about the companies and even read earnings reports. Refer to PacificCapital.com/SmartNotSpoiled for more resources.

CHAPTER 2

———

BORROW WISELY

"Those who understand interest earn it; those who don't, pay it."

—ALBERT EINSTEIN

When it comes to teaching kids about money so they grow up smart and not spoiled, there's a lot to cover. One key concept that even some adults need to learn is that there's a big difference between being able to afford something and being able to afford the payments on something. Consumers these days are overly obsessed with monthly payments, and that's a big reason why in February 2021, US consumer debt increased at an annual rate of 7.9 percent to slightly above $4.2 trillion. Personal debt has increased over the last decade to break all-time spending records. Understanding the cost of borrowing money is essential to be a financially successful adult—which is why you should teach it to your kids to understand this today. Let's look at how to start and what you could say.

Start with the basics when you explain this principle to your kids. First things first: loans represent money you receive from someone else with the agreement to pay it back. Usually, you must repay borrowed funds with interest, meaning as a borrower, you pay a certain percentage above the original loan amount you were given. That interest compensates the lender for loaning the money because they are now unable to use that money for anything else.

Teach your kids to be prudent and wise while borrowing and, if possible, to borrow money for purchases that go up in value, not down. Avoid the trap of what everyone else is doing and don't borrow money for personal spending. For instance, borrowing money to go out to eat at restaurants, to buy electronics and toys, clothing, or go to the movies is not ideal and should be avoided. You might borrow money to go to college, because a degree could increase your future earning power (hopefully) and represents an investment in yourself. You borrow for a house because you want somewhere to live, and houses tend to increase in value over time. By contrast, don't encourage your kids to borrow money from you or a relative to buy the latest gaming system, for example, because it's for relatively short-term entertainment and decreases in value over time. Teach your kids that borrowing money to buy anything increases the cost of that purchase. For example, borrowing $500,000 for a 30-year mortgage loan with a 5 percent annual interest rate makes the cost much higher than simply the $500,000 borrowed. Paying that loan over thirty years will nearly double the cost of the purchase to $966,278.92. Read that again.

PARENT TIP

Be very careful before you cosign a loan for your child. I believe cosigning is often more dangerous than it is helpful. Does it teach your kids to be smart or spoiled? Does it help them create their own financial independence? You will need to answer those questions yourself, but here are a few of the risks to consider before cosigning a loan for your child:

- You are responsible for the entire loan amount
- Your credit is on the line
- Your access to credit may be affected
- You could be sued by the lender
- Your relationship could be hurt if circumstances change for the worse
- The upside of cosigning a loan for someone is obvious: you can help them qualify for college tuition, a credit card, or some other financial product they could not get on their own. Or you could save them interest with a lower rate. However, proceed very cautiously. I have seen more troubled outcomes than successes when it comes to family members cosigning on loans for each other.

WHAT DO I TEACH MY KIDS ABOUT THE DIFFERENT TYPES OF LOANS?

We've all had to borrow money for something in our lives, and our children are no different. Begin by teaching them the basics—that there are many different types of loans and ways to borrow money. The most common loan types are mortgages, student loans, business loans, home equity loans, and car loans.

- **Mortgages** are money borrowed from a bank to help pay for a real estate property, such as a home. Most families need to borrow money to buy a home because the total cost is more than what you have ready in your bank account.
- **Student loans** pay for education. They can take a long time to pay off, following you into your thirties and beyond. This is why it's imperative to help your child consider the return on investment for a degree in their chosen field. Help them choose something marketable *and* enjoyable, not one or the other.

> ### PARENT TIP
>
> If you're funding your kids' education, pay attention to the degree they're after. I've had clients whose kids made big mistakes and borrowed too much money for fancy degrees like art history from expensive private universities when they could have received a comparable education at another institution for a quarter of the price.

- **Business loans** can take various forms. Kickstarter offers an alternative to traditional loans for budding entrepreneurs. Kickstarter is a New York–based crowd funding company founded in 2009 that exists to "help bring creative projects to life," according to its stated mission. Many young people get their first funding for their ideas through the platform. A traditional business loan is more relevant once you've established a business, hired employees, generated sales and revenues, and reached a point where you want to expand. Getting such a loan requires a solid business plan. The process represents a serious commitment, so such loans aren't to get started but rather to expand on established enterprises. As a growing entrepreneur, you can also look into SBA loans from the US Small Business Administration. The SBA has been around since 1953 and has a goal to help small business owners get the money they need to start and grow their companies. For many younger people, Kickstarter offers a great option, though it's important to note that not everyone who launches a campaign meets its funding goal. One way you could teach your kids about a business loan would be to have them create a simple business plan for their moneymaking venture over the next summer and approach you for a loan for some of the startup costs. For example, if your little children are going to have a lemonade and cookie stand, you might loan them money to buy the ingredients up front and then ask them to pay you back with interest once their sale is complete.

- **Home equity loans** or home equity lines of credit (HELOCs) are loans that banks offer when there's a big difference between what your home is worth and how much you owe on your mortgage loan. The bank may offer you a loan on a portion of that difference, called the equity, which is the net ownership value of your home. Use such loans cautiously, if at all. Too many people use HELOCs for wants rather than needs. For some reason, they see the equity as "extra money."

However, the truth is you'll have to pay it back, just like any other loan. So, using a HELOC to finance expensive, temporary wants is not wise. Teach your kids that a home equity line of credit is best viewed as an emergency brake option, not as some kind of slush fund to withdraw from when you want to buy toys and have some home equity (refer back to the history of overborrowing in 2005–2007 that led to a massive recession when real estate values crashed).

- **Car loans** are common in America, but I won't say I always see them used smartly. As stated earlier in this chapter, Americans today tend to think about spending in terms of monthly payments instead of the actual cost of what they're buying. Next time you're in a dealership looking to buy a new car, listen to the sales rep try to focus you on the monthly payment instead of the total cost of the car. You've got to step back and take a longer-term view; stay focused on the total cost. Lower monthly payments often mean *more* payments for more years, which means spending more on interest over time. As a result, the total cost is much higher than if you made the purchase outright. Imagine buying a Range Rover for $100,000, for instance, just because you can stretch out the payments over eight years. I remember as newlyweds living in our apartment complex here in Southern California and driving our old, used Honda. Our little Honda was surrounded by luxury cars in the apartment complex parking lot. I couldn't believe it, to be honest. Too many people rationalize overpaying. They have fancy, expensive cars they cannot really afford, simply because they're stretching to make the minimum monthly payment. Borrowing money to buy what you can't afford is not a good use of credit. Teaching your kids this early can save them a great amount of heartache and headache down the line. Of course, talking about this is only part of the teaching; you've got to actually show them by your own spending habits for the lesson to sink in.

WHAT DO I TEACH MY KIDS ABOUT CREDIT CARDS?

Part of the reason I believe the younger generation is often referred to as "entitled" today is because they've been raised around plastic currency. It's not their fault. It's everywhere.

They see you swipe a card, and that's it. The magic of money and consumption seems so easy to a child. If you never explain where that money comes from or why you're paying that way, it's not surprising that many kids grow up today with a loose grasp of what it means to earn and spend responsibly.

You can start to fix that, at least in your own home, by teaching your kids about credit cards.

Start by explaining that credit cards represent another way of borrowing money. In 2019, for the first time ever, personal credit card debt in the US exceeded $1 trillion. The average family has around $8,000 in credit card debt, with an average interest rate of 18 percent per year. Some cards make you pay a rate as high as 35 percent. Your kids will see you using credit cards or will know that you are ordering things online with your credit card, so it's important for them to understand the responsibility that use entails. They should also know the moment they turn eighteen, they'll begin receiving credit card solicitations from every financial institution under the sun.

I wrestle with whether credit cards are ever a good idea, even when used "responsibly." Many of my family members and friends love credit cards for the points and rewards. Some of them justify it because they pay the bill off every month, avoiding the cost of any interest. However, the challenge I have with advocating for credit cards for everyday spending is because people simply spend more money when they use a credit card.

Psychological research and studies show that people spend as much as 113 percent more when using a credit card compared to when they use cash or a debit card. People perceive purchases made with credit cards differently than those made with cash or debit cards, whether because the payment is delayed, they know they don't have to pay the full amount, or some other reason. In the end, I don't personally believe the points and rewards make up for that loose overspending.

We stopped using our personal credit cards in 2006 and haven't used one since. We do use a business credit card as it is required in some cases. I recognize I'm rare in that choice to not use credit cards as a family, but I think it's an important one. I'm aware that there are financial gurus on both sides of this argument and there are many things to be said, which we won't get into in this book; we're here to teach your kids.

Maybe you have a perfect record of paying your card off for sixty years with no interest, but the studies still show that you'll spend more, as much as double the amount you would have otherwise. Credit cards simply make it easier to buy things you can't currently afford to pay for. The less friction there is in buying things, the easier it becomes to spend.

The New York Times published an article titled "Credit Cards Encourage Extra Spending as the Cash Habit Fades Away," which noted the following illogical behavior:

> When you vary the payment method, people are willing to pay more. You're not forking over an actual dollar bill, so there is less sensation of loss…When credit cards were an option…MBA students offered to pay roughly twice as much as they were willing to hand over in cash for the same tickets.

Think of why companies (and casinos) make you use chips, tokens, membership cards, wristbands, etc. to spend money at their business. There's a reason for that! The bottom line? Ensure your kids understand that credit cards do help you build credit and allow for some flexibility if your income is variable, but there is a real risk attached to using it for everyday spending. Still, make no mistake: credit cards are a form of borrowing money, and they have an added cost, often a very expensive one. Even if the only cost is the temptation to spend more money, there's still a cost.

> "My wife and I were discussing interest rates, credit card debt, and how best to pay them down. Our eleven-year-old heard the conversation and said, 'What is debt?" What is interest?' In that moment, we realized we have to teach our kids about these things when they're young. We can't wait any longer."
>
> —ADAM KRUEGER, DIRECTOR OF OPERATIONS
> AND SAFETY, AMERICO BUILDERS

WHAT DO I TEACH MY KIDS ABOUT INTEREST RATES?

First of all, your kids need to understand different loan types have vastly different interest rates, apply to different dollar amounts, and vary in their payoff timelines. The rates depend on many different factors, including your personal credit score, your credit history (how good you've been at paying back loans in the past), and how affordable the purchase is, based on your financial situation.

It also matters whether you have collateral, something the lender can legally take from you if you don't pay the loan back. Interest rates are lower on loans for your house or car, because the bank has something valuable to repossess if you don't pay them. They're higher on credit cards, because as the borrower, you don't necessarily promise to give the credit card company things you bought if you are late or delinquent on your loan payments. The higher the risk for the lender, the more they will charge you in fees and interest.

Teach your child to pay attention to what the annual percentage rate (APR) is on a given loan and talk about the fact that most loans come with additional costs, besides the interest charged. Just to get the loan established, you'll have to pay some extra fees, which makes the actual cost higher than what the bank quotes you.

FIXED VS. VARIABLE INTEREST RATES

This concept is for your older kids: interest rates can be fixed or variable. When interest rates are generally low, it's a great opportunity to consider longer-term fixed-rate loans versus variable ones. In early- to mid-2021, the average thirty-year mortgage rate was around 2.7 percent APR. The average small business bank loan rate was 5 percent, but the range is between 3 percent and 7 percent. Rates for federal loans issued between July 1, 2020, and June 30, 2021, will be 2.75 percent for undergraduate Stafford Loans, according to the May Treasury auction, down from 4.53 percent this year. Work with your kids to compare those numbers to the rates at the time you're reading this book.

If a loan's rate is fixed, it stays the same for the entire period of the loan. Fixed-rate loans have the benefit of predictability. You know exactly what your monthly payment of principal and interest will be every month. There are few downsides to these loans compared to a variable rate, unless you expect interest rates to drop significantly, in which case it would be better to borrow with a variable-rate loan. In that situation, though, you might be able to refinance after interest rates decline anyway. On the flip side, the bank may charge you a higher rate if it expects interest rates to rise over time. Because you start out at that higher rate, you could end up paying more up front than you otherwise would.

Fixed-rate loans protect you from rising interest rates, and you'll know the total cost of borrowing up front, allowing you to budget, plan, and make better, more informed choices about whether the cost of borrowing is worth it. Overall, fixed-rate loans carry less risk because of their predictability.

Until 1980, interest rates consistently rose. People still talk about when their mortgage rate was 16 percent per year. However, since 1980, they've been falling essentially for forty straight years. The trend line is a massive mountain peak like Mount Everest, which peaked in 1980. At the time of this writing in 2021, rates are basically zero. They've never been lower in United States history than they are today. This is excellent for people borrowing long-term loans, but terrible for people who are saving money and trying to earn interest in their fixed-income investment accounts.

- 30-Year Fixed Rate Mortgage Average in the United States
- 30-Year Treasury Constant Maturity Rate
- 10-Year Treasury Constant Maturity Rate
- 5-Year Treasury Constant Maturity Rate
- 1-Year Treasury Constant Maturity Rate
- Effective Federal Funds Rate

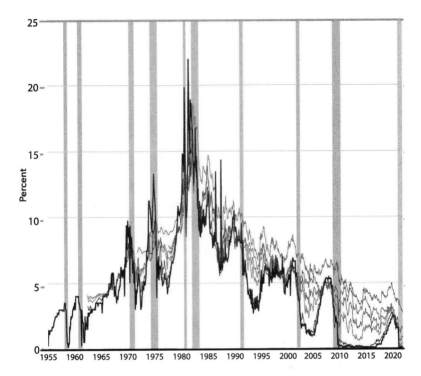

Variable-rate loans typically change on a predetermined schedule, and they're often tied to a particular financial index. For example, the rate might change every three months. Some loans change every month, while others adjust annually. Some mortgages are fixed for five years and then switch to variable. Variable loans have clearly defined terms but with a range of potential change, so you'll know in advance how frequently the rate will change and what the cap is, limiting how high (or low) it can move at once. The bank can't suddenly change the rate without warning, but rates certainly can and will change over time. Helping your kids understand that interest rates change and they matter is a great place to start.

> *"You must gain control over your money, or the lack of it will forever control you."*
>
> —DAVE RAMSEY

WHAT DO I TEACH MY KIDS ABOUT THE PITFALLS OF BORROWING RECKLESSLY?

You set your kids up for serious trouble if you avoid teaching them about the potential major pitfalls of borrowing money recklessly. What do they think happens if you don't pay their loans back? Do they know? Ask them, then explain that the consequences are very serious, including bankruptcy, losing your house, losing your car, and not being able to borrow money when you need to in the future. In many situations, lenders can take money directly out of your paycheck or your bank account without permission if you don't pay back your loans.

There's no universal formula to figure out how much a person should borrow in a given period of time, but make sure you're only borrowing money for specific, necessary purchases. Borrowing is not bad or wrong on its own, but it needs to be done with intention and purpose. Borrowing money for investments and for your private businesses can be a great way to build wealth, but I strongly recommend you only do that within the context of a thoughtful financial plan. In any case, do not borrow more than you need to, because you'll have to pay back the money with interest and fees. When kids come to the Bank of Mom or Dad and the money supply appears to be unlimited, they may get used to that feeling of free and easy money for whatever their heart desires. I find the most conflict comes when kids want to impulsively buy something, and the Bank of Mom or Dad is closed for business. Have you ever had that happen in your family? The emotions of anger and disappointment come out on full display because that impulsive desire to buy something isn't immediately satisfied.

Help your kids ask these clarifying questions: When looking at the total cost of borrowing and the purchase price, is this something I really need? Does it make sense to buy this particular car or house based on what I can truly afford? Does it make sense to go to this particular university, based on its current tuition and the income I might realistically earn from a job or career using my intended degree?

A common saying in my field is "Quick to borrow is always slow to pay." In other words, if you're impulsive about taking on debt, you likely don't have a reliable plan to pay it back. If you really want to teach your kids about expensive loans, spend some time discussing a "payday loan." Payday loans prey on those impulses by offering quick money but charging exorbitant interest and fees for the convenience. Such loans are extremely expensive. The key point of this chapter is to help kids learn to respect the responsibility of credit and approach borrowing with care and caution.

As stated earlier, most Americans look at monthly payments on all manner of loans and subscription services without ever considering what they're actually paying. Not all such services are bad, but you need to make financial decisions by understanding how much purchases cost, not just how much the monthly payment is if you borrow and stretch the payments over many years into your future. Lenders and salespeople play games and stretch the payment out as far as they can. Car loans never used to go out seven or eight years, but now such terms are common. Dealers realize if they make the loans longer, the individual payments get smaller, and people will rationalize the higher total cost. Similarly, mortgages used to be for ten or fifteen years, and now the standard is thirty years. Some are even going out for forty years!

I don't want to give the wrong impression: not all borrowing is bad. Many of my clients have loans—they're not all debt-free. However, the approach to spending and borrowing matters if you want to avoid stress and heartache around finances. Before you borrow, you need to plan, prepare, and think through whether you truly need to borrow and how you'll pay off the loan. Impulsive borrowing causes problems, as does borrowing for luxuries you can't afford—kids should know early on to avoid borrowing in those situations. Tell them, yes, but also teach by example. If they see you put impulse purchases on credit cards all the time, that example will provide their blueprint and expectations for the future.

DO TRY THIS AT HOME: LEARNING ACTIVITIES

Try the following with your kids to open up conversations about loans and borrowing.

The Real-Life Game of Life. If you have kids ages twelve or older, walk through an exercise of a home purchase, starting with finding a property on Zillow. (Hint: there's a great *Marketplace* segment you can draw from titled "Who Thought 30-Year

Mortgages Were a Good Thing?"*) You can do a similar exercise with a car purchase, using a website like Autotrader. We are going through this experience right now as my sixteen-year-old is looking at cars. She is going to put some of her modest savings as the down payment on a used car and is figuring out how she might finance the rest of the purchase, if needed. The research time she is putting into different used car options provides us so many conversations and learning opportunities. Side note: it's really opened her eyes to see and calculate the additional costs of gasoline, car insurance, and other car maintenance costs she is estimating.

Borrow In-House. Set up an actual loan agreement and repayment plan if/when your teen wants money for a big-ticket item. By charging them interest, you can show them the implications of borrowing. They'll have firsthand experience with how it works and be more prepared when they're living on their own. You can also "borrow" fifty dollars or a similar small sum from your teen and pay it back with interest over a few weeks. You can work out the payment schedule and interest owed. That way, they'll have the experience of collecting money and know what it feels like to be both a borrower and a lender. If they only hear about these concepts, it won't ever sink in. They need to actually practice the financial concepts to learn what they need to learn.

Simplify with Candy or Treats. With younger kids, you can explain the concept of debt quite simply using something they want—like candy or another type of treat. If they have a stash in their room, for example, tell them they can have one now for instant gratification—*if* they give you two back later.

---

* https://www.marketplace.org/2013/11/25/who-thought-30-year-mortgages-were-good-thing/

Bring Them with You. The next time you are meeting with a lender for a home purchase or refinance, include your children in some of the conversation. Bring them with you to the bank. If you are buying a car and looking at different car options at a dealership or used car lot, bring your kids with you. Have them help you calculate the different costs and also the loan amounts required to pay for the car. It's a great experience that they will remember for a very long time.

Put It in Writing. If you're loaning your older kids money for a larger purchase, have them repay you with interest. Put this in writing, including a payment plan and terms. Write up a real contract and state the consequences of nonpayment. This is important because if you loan your child money without charging interest, that can teach them a false reality and help create a dependency you don't want later on.

CHAPTER 3

KNOW YOUR CASH FLOW

"Cash flow tells the story of how a person handles money."

—KHAN HAYAT

If you don't tell your money where to go, it will tell you where to go. Most of us were never taught how to track or manage our income and expenses, so we end up just winging it. One day, we have a bank account and a job and off we go.

The truth? It'll be the same for your kids if you don't teach them properly.

Know this: your kids are never really too young to learn about budgeting and personal financial planning. You can talk to your little ones about money when in line at the grocery store, and how you've planned to earn and save money so your family could buy this food for the upcoming week. No matter how much money you earn, you need to keep track of it and understand where it goes. Having a clear picture of your financial life helps avoid the huge mistakes most people make. With technology these days, it's never been easier to track your spending and your income. There are countless free apps to help you with this, but even the banks themselves do a decent job showing you where your money is going every month. Showing your kids that there is some thought and intention behind your spending and budgeting (assuming there actually is) will teach them to be smart and intentional with the money they earn.

Running out of money during the month is a real possibility for people who neglect personal financial planning. If you don't pay attention to your money at all and have no awareness of where it's going, you're headed for trouble. This is why banks offer you overdraft protection and credit cards to back up your checking account. (PS: they make a lot of money from the fees and charges you incur when you have to tap into these resources after overspending for the month.) You might need to scare your kids a little bit and explain the consequences of reckless financial behavior. Like most adults, kids may think that impulsive spending behavior could be solved if you just figure out a way to earn more money. Nothing could be further from the truth! As I've shared with my own children, people's spending habits often are like the vines that become overgrown and take over the fence or the house until it's completely out of control. Your habits of overspending will not be solved when your income goes up. Those habits cause you to simply increase your indulgent spending! You could spend five minutes on the internet to show your kids how many celebrities and pro athletes who have earned hundreds of millions of dollars have ended up being completely broke and financially bankrupt.

As we discussed with borrowing, failing to budget and plan financially can lead to bankruptcy, losing your house, and other life-altering consequences. These stories are all too common. Forty-four percent of Americans don't have enough cash to cover a $400 emergency, but such unexpected, emergency expenses happen all the time. On the flip side, planning your cash flow and knowing your budget will give you a strong sense of confidence when making financial decisions. You will be more prepared and feel more steady in your life when you are intentional with your money…even when accidents happen. My advice to you would be to take the next situation of an unexpected expense and turn it into a teaching moment with your kids. If we get a cracked windshield, a flat tire, a broken dishwasher, or a leak in our roof, we will share with our kids what the repair expenses were and how that wasn't part of our planned budget. Teach your kids to expect these kinds of situations to come up; it's real life. The more knowledgeable your kids are about financial planning today, the better they'll be set up to handle emergency expenses in the future.

> *"A budget is telling your money where to go instead of wondering where it went."*
>
> —JOHN MAXWELL

WHAT DO I TEACH MY KIDS ABOUT CASH FLOW?

Money in general can be a touchy topic, and the word "budget" can be especially loaded. It might make you feel restricted and think about the scarcity and limitations of not being able to buy or do what you want. I know most people are averse to budgeting—it sounds like tedious homework. A lot of this depends on how you were raised and what habits, examples, and words were used when talking about money. I'm trying to prepare my kids to be smart with money in the future. In my own family and with my clients, I prefer to use the actual business terms "personal income statement and balance sheet." Whatever you call it, though, kids growing into young adults need to know their numbers and keep track of their cash flow, which means understanding how much money is coming in and going out.

If kids learn how to make a personal income statement and balance sheet while still in school, they'll have a tremendous advantage in their future. You need a grasp of those skills for both business and your personal life. If your teenage child works many hours and earns thirty dollars, they may think twice about going out to a restaurant and a movie and seeing that cash flow disappear in a flash. I encourage you to use the terminology and teach your kids these words so that they're not foreign to them in their future careers. For example, they can learn that an "income statement" is just the fancy professional way businesses refer to a budget over a specific period of time. It spells out all the sources of income, all the expenses, and how much is left over at the end of the time period. The balance sheet shows what you own and what you owe at a specific point in time. For families, a balance sheet might also be called a "net worth statement." An income statement covers a period of time, such as a monthly or yearly income statement, while a balance sheet provides more of a snapshot at a specific point in time. CASHFLOW for Kids, the board game I suggested previously, includes the use of personal income statements and personal balance sheets. I've found that kids learn better by doing and by experiencing (like playing a board game in this example) rather than just being talked at. Someday a bank will likely ask your grown children for their personal balance sheet or an income statement, and they will be glad you taught them all of this when they were young.

Here's another good way to initiate a good discussion with your kids about cash flow: ask them to describe how it feels when they receive money. Their eyes will light up. I bet they smile as they describe what it feels like. You might also discuss the difference of how it feels when money is gifted to them (like for their birthday) versus when they've worked really hard to earn money on their own. Either way, help them acknowledge the feelings attached to receiving and spending money. This will prepare them to be more aware of their own money habits in the future.

This stuff really matters. Too many people don't want to face the cold, hard facts. They don't want to know the truth about where their money's going. They just want do what they please, without paying too much attention to the cost of their Netflix subscription, Peloton bike, food delivery services, gym membership, or any other monthly expenses. I understand. It's more fun and easier to spend money without the hassle of discussing it with anyone or tracking what we spend. There's nothing wrong with any of these things we spend money on (I love my Peloton, for instance), but we need to be more aware of what we are doing with our money situation each month.

Almost no one I talk to really knows how much they spend on a monthly basis. Regardless of their income level, 95 percent or more have no accurate picture of what's going on. I've talked about this with young families earning $4,000 per month and also clients making as much as $25 million in one year. Most of the time, people aren't sure how much they spend. Kids, in turn, almost never know how much their parents spend on them or how much their family's lifestyle costs. We can't really blame them if we as parents don't know it ourselves. As mentioned earlier, my sixteen-year-old daughter now has her driver's license and is preparing to buy a used car. She's becoming even more aware of how much it costs to fill up a car with gas or pay for car insurance, or even the parking costs at school or the beach. It's especially painful that the price at the pump has nearly doubled in the last few months; we paid $127 to fill up my wife's SUV this past weekend! But these are great lessons for her as she obtains more freedom through more responsibility in her life.

Even if tracking cash flow and planning feels tedious to you, it's critical if you want to reach any of your goals that cost money. You will not reach financial success on accident. So much of what you want to do now and in the future has a price attached, so if those goals are important to you, it should also be important to you to make progress toward them by sticking to a plan.

"We own a small family franchise business. My oldest (five years old) will help Grandpa some days and gets very excited about earning tips from customers. He will give her the tips to bring home. She always wants to spend the money right away on a toy. The first thing she said the other day was, 'Daddy I want to buy a toy at the store right now. Can we go?' That gave us a chance to have a conversation about the following:

1. *We first tithe 10 percent to God.*

2. *We don't spend everything we make; we save some of it.*

3. *With the money left after those two things, you can purchase something because you earned it.*

4. *When you are good at what you do and treat customers nicely and respectfully, you make more money (better tips).*

"I'm also fortunate to have a young fourteen-year-old boy I mentor, who has taken ownership of a small part of the business. He is learning the same principles while helping provide for his household with a hardworking single mother. It's been very rewarding to watch his growth and courage as a young man. He is saving for a car when he turns sixteen, and I can't wait to watch him purchase it!"

—LUKE FRESHWATER, MBA, US ARMY
VETERAN, REGIONAL SALES MANAGER

WHAT DO I TEACH MY KIDS ABOUT BUDGETING?

All that being said, budgets per se rarely work because people don't exercise enough discipline to track and monitor all of their income and expenses. Most financial advisors will say you need a traditional budget, but I actually suggest you choose what method works best for you and your family. If you are one of those people who feels restricted by budgets and won't stick to them, I've got a different idea for you. Here's what you need to do instead: decide on a specific dollar amount to save/invest every month and make that automatic transfer right away when you get paid, every time. Have that money come off the top automatically. Stick to your savings and investing goals every week or month, and then do what you want with the rest of your income. The only downside to this approach is if you spend more than you have in your account. I'm not an advocate for credit cards, as you know if you've read this far. Put plainly, if you have $200 left in your account, don't go buy something for $300. I've seen couples who used to argue about their budget adopt this style and have much more harmony in their home around money. The spouse who was prone to budget and track expenses (that's probably you, since your spouse wouldn't have picked up this book to read) was less stressed about everything because their monthly savings goal was already achieved. You still need to keep an eye out for how much is left in your account, but it's not as rigid as a traditional budget might feel. This may be a more motivating way of "budgeting" that your kids can latch onto. For example, if your eleven-year-old daughter has a goal to save fifty dollars a month and she feels free to spend anything she earns above that fifty dollars, then she may be more incentivized to find ways to earn money above that fifty-dollar savings goal for the month, rather than saying "you can only spend ten dollars at a restaurant and twenty dollars at the movies this month."

If your own personal goal is to save $500, $5,000, or even $50,000 a month, then as soon as you hit that goal at the beginning of the month, you don't need to stress about every little spending category going forward. Just note what you have left to spend, and don't exceed that amount. You don't have to make exhaustive lists in a detailed spreadsheet. This different approach gives people way more mental freedom and is easier to understand—especially for kids. We don't want to make this feel like an anxiety-inducing homework assignment. Personal cash flow planning doesn't have to be a restrictive chore. If done right, it will actually build confidence and help you feel more stability in your daily life.

You've probably heard some of these life mottos: You can live better if you're living on purpose. If you don't control your day, the day controls you. **If you don't control your money, your money controls you.** Living intentionally matters. My number one philosophy on budgeting is you need to pay yourself first. Don't pay your bills first; put some investment and savings money away for your future first, and then pay your bills with what's left over. Teach your kids to prioritize securing their future by saving and investing first. This approach offers a way to budget without feeling like you're budgeting. If you have savings and investment goals and know the total amount of money you'll spend, then you don't necessarily need to track every little expense.

PARENT TIP

Recognize that your kids are growing up in a different time than you, one in which they probably want to "keep up with the Instagram Joneses," in some way. If kids have social media, they are constantly exposed to wealthy "influencers." You can't necessarily shield them from this new reality, but you can teach them the practical work behind those fancy items.

Kids see nice vacations and other amazing experiences on social media that they aspire to. In reality, you won't reach your financial goals and dreams by accident. You have to be intentional. Planning, preparation, attention, and some amount of sacrifice and delayed gratification are all part of the deal if you want financial freedom and security.

Your kids should know when they become adults and are out on their own, they can't instantly or automatically live the lifestyle you've been giving them. It takes parents time to build up their incomes and careers, expanding what they can afford over time. Many young people think they can skip the hard times of budgeting and being somewhat broke, because they see people on Instagram or TikTok who've made it big at a young age. Those images make living large look easy. In the real world, though, most people won't go viral and make millions of dollars overnight. You will likely need to put in some work and plan out your financial life to get where you're trying to go.

WHAT DO I TEACH MY KIDS ABOUT TRANSPARENCY AND MONEY?

Every family has a slightly different philosophy and comfort level regarding how much they share about finances with their children. What is your approach? Are your kids totally in the dark about how much things actually cost? If you don't share anything with them about money, think about how that affects your kids now and in the future. News flash: they will be as clueless about money as they are today; so it's time to make a change. Imagine your child graduating high school and entering adulthood and having no concept of what anything costs. That's not just embarrassing, that's dangerous.

I personally share the cost of everything. Over last Thanksgiving break, we went to Disneyworld in Orlando, Florida, for the first time ever. I let them know that the park entrance fees were $200 per person, plus the food and parking, making the visit $1,700 in one day. I asked them to think about how much work they'd have to do to earn $1,700 after taxes, just to go to an amusement park for one day and have some fun together. The next day we made our own lunches and brought them in our backpacks to the other amusement park instead of buying the food there. I believe that was because our kids realized how much money was being shelled out on their behalf. They were happy to help make the lunches and seemed much more appreciative of the experience.

Depending on your comfort level and your kids' age and maturity, you can share more or less—but overall, I don't see any upside to hiding the cost of what your family spends money on. Secrecy doesn't help them learn or become more responsible as they prepare to become adults. You're hurting your kids if you make money a taboo topic in your family. Ignorance will only harm them.

I understand keeping your own income confidential. You should at least review different careers with your teenagers and the potential education requirements, work life, and potential earnings of different careers. They don't necessarily need to know what your monthly paycheck is. However, if you go out for pizza, for example, it's good for kids to know the cost of that dinner. I'll tell my kids our dinner out for seven cost $150. By sharing such information, you can start to give them a sense of the cost of different activities in the world. Your kids can learn to be smart, not spoiled, once they recognize the contributions others are making in their young lives. They can appreciate the sacrifice you make on their behalf once you open up about it. My word of caution is to share these things and then add that it's a pleasure or a privilege to provide for them and that you do it because you love them. Never make them feel like a total cost or burden. Don't give them guilt for the money you spend to provide for them. That's not at all the point of sharing financial insights with your kids.

Of course, at the same time you have transparency in your own family, you can also teach the etiquette of not asking other people about money. **Good manners and financial literacy can go hand in hand**. I teach my kids not to ask a neighbor how much their car costs, but I also know all that information is available online anyway. One time while picking up my two older sons in their after-school carpool, my kids' little friend asked me how much my car cost because he said it's a fancy car. I was caught off guard. I quickly flipped it around and asked him what his guess was, and it turned out he had googled it already anyway. I had to laugh that a seven-year-old kid was looking up luxury cars online. Remember that kids these days have more information at their fingertips than we ever did, so transparency is really becoming necessary.

My approach is not to wait for my kids to ask. If you have open money conversations in your family, then your kids won't be as nosy and curious. They'll just be seeking to understand the world of money in the safe environment of your family conversations. If it's forbidden, they'll try to figure out the answers on their own or from unreliable sources, and they may get the wrong idea—or learn to avoid the topic entirely, to their own detriment. In my family growing up, we really didn't talk about money or sex, which didn't make those issues go away. I still was going to face these topics as an adult, and as a parent on my own. As I shared in the introduction of this book, parents are more willing to talk to their kids about drugs and sex than they are about money. Shocking, but true! You don't need to be overly blunt, but having age-appropriate conversations with your children will prepare them for living in the real world on their own. At least that way, you can pass on your values and knowledge, rather than leaving things up to chance or them hearing everything from other people who may have very different standards or values than your family.

> *"At age four or five, we give each kid three jars. One jar is for giving, one for saving, and one is for spending. We start them super early, and the amounts don't really matter so long as they understand the three basic functions of money. It's baby step number one."*
>
> **—SEAN WARD, SENIOR VICE PRESIDENT, CBRE**

WHAT DO I TEACH MY KIDS ABOUT ALLOWANCES?

Do your kids get an allowance? How much?

If you really want your kids to be smart and not spoiled, it might be time to rethink that decision.

This may be an unpopular answer to this common question, but I don't give my kids allowances. When they originally asked me why they don't an allowance and their friends do, I explained that money is something to be earned and appreciated. It didn't feel right to give my kids money just for existing; my wife and I don't want them growing up getting used to being paid for not doing anything specific. What are we really teaching them if they just get money every week because it's Saturday? It feels like that would create complacency and some dependency that we don't really want to encourage in our family. However, if they see the correlation between effort and earning money, they will build the resilience and mindset that is required to be a successful and independent adult. Once we explained the opportunities to earn money and why we feel strongly about this, our kids were on board with it.

> *"It's not how much money you make, but how much you keep, how hard it works for you, and how many generations you keep it for."*
>
> **—ROBERT KIYOSAKI**

Instead of paying an allowance, my wife and I have a "menu of earning opportunities" for our children to choose from. There are dozens of age-appropriate tasks that they can choose to complete and earn points for each one. Every Saturday morning, they turn in their work and get paid based on how many points they earned for the week. There is a lot of personal freedom and accountability that goes into this weekly exercise. Every day they get to decide how much work to put in and if they are really committed to reaching their goal for the week. This actually benefits them because instead of a fixed allowance payment, their earning potential isn't as limited and it's really up to them. Practically, if they work hard and seek out extra opportunities to earn money around the house, they can make much more than the twenty dollars a week their friends get. My fourteen-year-old son, Pierce, is saving for an electric scooter or a moped and has been working so hard this past month. He's earned over $400 in the past month and is getting close to his goal. It's very rewarding when you can see your kids put in hard work and stretch themselves in pursuit of a goal they are excited to reach! When they turn in their weekly worksheet, we get to discuss what lessons they learned and how they felt it went for the week. They are full of confidence and self-esteem when they turn in their worksheet and get paid for their effort. Below is an excerpt snapshot of our "menu of earning opportunities" that shows some of the one- and two-point tasks our kids can choose from:

Help Cook Family Breakfast or Family Dinner	1
Do Additional Helper (Get Approval First)	1
Write and Give a Personal Thank-You Card	1
Complete Your Helper for the Day	1
Journal (Video or Written)	1
Draw/Color/Work on an Arts or Crafts Project	1
Help Younger Sibling with Homework	1
Fill Up Front Fountain, Then Roll Up Hose	1
Make Bed Right When You Wake Up	1
Morning "I AM" Statements in Morning and Evening	1
Clean Room and Bathroom (Nothing on Floor, Counter)	1
Do a Kind Act of Service for Neighbor	1
Pump Up All Sports Balls	1
Clean Entire Piano	1
Wipe Pool House Counters	1
20 Minutes of Typing Practice (typingagent.com)	2
Write about Something Interesting (Paragraph Form)	2
20 Minutes of Family History Indexing	2
Wash/Dry/Fold Your Laundry or Mom's/Dad's Laundry	2
Windex All Gym Mirrors	2
Vacuum Parents' Bathroom Rug and Closet Carpet	2
Windex 10 Kitchen Windows	2
Wash All 7 Bikes	2
Wipe Down All Gym Equipment and Weights	2
Watch Educational YouTube Vid (Dad Approved)	2
Watch or Listen to Something in Spanish for 20 Minutes	2

Our approach teaches the kids to make choices regarding how much work they want to put in based on their goals. If they want to buy something specific for Christmas or pay their way at Disneyland with friends, then they can come to us with the amount they need and find out how to earn it. If they want to go to a birthday party, they know they've got to earn money to buy a gift for their friend. Imagine the sense of self-confidence and independence your kids feel when they hand over the present to their friends that they purchased with their own hard work. Even our five- and seven-year-olds, Beckham and Bentley, do some chores and "helpers" to earn some money and contribute to the gifts they give out at birthday parties. They also get creative and sometimes look for opportunities to make additional money to buy a toy of their own. They'll ask if they can earn a certain amount for washing all the windows and cleaning out the garage, for example, and we'll negotiate.

If you use this commission-based earnings approach, you'll find that when your kids are lazy, they don't earn much, which offers a real-life lesson in itself. If you don't work, it's hard to earn money. Maybe you've asked your kids to earn and pay their own way to the movies, but they don't really feel motivated to work. If their friends are going and they don't have the money, missing out will likely prompt them to apply themselves more next time.

Don't get me wrong. We still spend plenty on our kids as far as gifts and treats, believe me, but they don't get everything they ask for. They need to make some investment in or contribution to the bigger items they want to acquire. Some families have a fixed allowance for a fixed number of chores every week, but I like that our system allows for more choice, responsibility, accountability, and initiative.

> *"My kids enjoyed playing the Lego video games on our Xbox. As part of the game, you gather little coins that can be spent later on other characters or vehicles, etc. My youngest would ask, 'Can we buy X?' and I'd have him look at our balance. I'd ask him if we had enough. I'm not a huge proponent of lots of video games, but since we were playing it, I took the time to teach a lesson.*
>
> *"My daughter loved to play 'café,' where she would prepare fake meals for us, bring out plates, and act as our waitress. At first, we just played along. Eventually, though, we took it a step further and had her create a menu, complete with pricing. When she was able, we'd ask her to add up the cost of everything we'd ordered for a grand total. After I'd grab my wallet and tell her to 'run my card,' we'd talk about the different types of cards and whether I was using my money or 'someone else's money' to pay for the meal. Over months and months of playtime, we still got some lessons in there."*
>
> —ISAAC BROWN, MBA, PROCESS IMPROVEMENT
> LEADER, NORTHBAY HEALTHCARE

DO TRY THIS AT HOME: FAMILY ACTIVITIES

Try the following with your kids to open up conversations about budgeting and financial planning.

There's an App for That. The idea of budgeting can be overwhelming, but the micro process of tracking how much your family spends is actually quite simple. There are many different apps that can help you track your expenses and monitor your bank account cash flow. Some popular examples (at the time of this writing) include Mint, Pocketguard, Goodbudget, and Honeydue. You can simply check your phone to see how much you spend and have a productive family discussion based on the mini reports in your app. If you don't want to go the app route, most banks have a feature allowing you to get a breakdown of expenses by category. If you have an existing account, you can run a report. For instance, the Chase and Wells Fargo apps offer a free spending summary report that automatically categorizes all your expenses for the year or month. It's very convenient and offers a great starting point to start an important conversation with your kids.

Track Expenses Together. Have your kids track their expenses and income for three months. Have them use a spreadsheet or get out the old-fashioned pencil and paper. Then, let them see the expenses of the household. You could even put them in charge of monitoring it for three months. They'll have a greater appreciation for you as a parent when they see the real numbers, and they'll have a ballpark for how much basics—food, clothing, insurance, gas, electricity—will actually cost when they're older.

Go to the Bank Together. If your kids are ten or older, open a checking account and get them a debit card for kids—one which you will, of course, monitor. Have them do their own financial planning and save for purchases, large and small. The act of having the responsibility can make them feel mature and therefore more excited to participate. Here is a picture from March 15, 2014, when my then nine-year-old daughter, McKinley, and six-year-old son, Pierce, opened and funded their first bank account:

♥ Q ▽ 🔖

 Liked by **momentswitht** and **22 others**

mr_seadubb Big day. Opened their own bank accounts funded on their own from their neighborhood business. They now have their own online logins and debit cards! Gotta teach them young how to be smart with 💰💰

View all 2 comments

March 15, 2014

CHAPTER 4

TALKING TAXES

"What's the difference between a taxidermist and a tax collector?
The taxidermist only takes your skin."

—MARK TWAIN

Ann Landers said, "A person doesn't know how much he has to be thankful for until he has to pay taxes on it." And boy—isn't that true.

Taxes are the biggest budget expense you'll have in your entire life, but most people don't think about them until the bill comes due. Hardly anyone budgets for taxes. They think their biggest expense is their rent or mortgage, but it's not. Every time money changes hands in a transaction, taxes are due. They're a fact of life, and to be financially successful, you must factor them in and plan ahead. Kids need a basic understanding of taxes so they aren't completely caught off guard. Learning will help them be better prepared financially.

WHAT DO I TEACH MY KIDS ABOUT TYPES OF TAXES?

Sales tax is usually the first kind of tax children experience directly. They often wonder why, if they have a five-dollar bill, it won't be enough to buy something with a price tag of $4.99. The answer is sales tax. This tax differs by city, state, and county. In some places, like Oregon, there might be zero sales tax (Alaska, Delaware, Montana, New Hampshire, and Oregon all do not impose a sales tax). In others, it might be 9 to 10 percent. As of today, Tennessee has the highest sales tax rate with 9.55 percent.

I've traveled internationally with my kids to countries where the value-added tax (VAT), which is similar to a sales tax, is as high as 20 percent. If you go to a restaurant and get a bill for one hundred dollars, you have a tip of 15–20 percent to add on and then they also automatically add a 20 percent tax on top of it.

Because taxes differ across locations, if you're making a big purchase like a car, you might want to look at where you're purchasing it. You may be able to get the same car from a place that has 0 percent sales tax versus 10 percent, which can save lots of money. Keep in mind that there are approximately 10,000 sales tax jurisdictions in the US, including cities, counties, and other districts, and each jurisdiction has its own tax laws. You may have to pay local taxes on top of state ones. Buying something expensive like a car could have many different taxes and fees depending on where you are buying it and registering it. Consult a CPA for how the tax rules apply to you and your situation.

Teach your kids that taxes are a part of nearly everything you own or buy or earn. If you own a property, like a house or an office building, you must pay property taxes on it every year, just for owning it. When you earn income from a job or investment, you pay taxes on that, too.

You're taxed on what you earn, sell, and buy—and sometimes even when you die. If you have accumulated more than a certain threshold of wealth (this threshold number seems to change every few years), then when you die, 40 to 50 percent of what you have doesn't go to your spouse, kids, or grandkids; it goes to the government. Up to 50 percent! Talk about people rolling in their graves. This tax doesn't affect most American families, but it's still painful for those it does affect. There is talk in 2021 to greatly increase the number of families affected by this family estate tax. There are proposals to cut the tax-free inheritance allowed by as much as 75 percent!

Inheritance tax is what that's called—the tax on the assets and the wealth passed to the next generation when you die. The rate and the amount to be taxed depend on the tax and estate planning laws at the time. They constantly change, depending on who the president is, where you live, and a few other factors. Those numbers remain fluid, never staying the same for more than five or ten years, because different political parties believe such taxes should be lower or higher.

> *"If you put the federal government in charge of the Sahara Desert, in five years there'd be a shortage of sand."*
>
> —MILTON FRIEDMAN

WHAT DO I TEACH MY KIDS ABOUT TAX DIFFERENCES IN STATES?

When you earn money in the United States, you pay taxes to the federal government, which help fund basic services and protections, from equipping the US military to maintaining roads, etc. It's good for kids to understand that some of the money they make goes toward the state and federal government, not as a punishment, but to pay for different programs and services. Voters help decide what those programs are and how much gets spent. If kids understand how the process works, then they're more likely to see voting as important, too, in order to have an influence on what they think are and are not good uses of their tax dollars.

Federal tax laws apply to you no matter what state you live in. However, each state has their own tax rules. Recently, during the COVID pandemic where most people were forced to work from home, many people were leaving high-income-tax states to move to low- or no-income-tax states. They figure that if they're not going to an office anymore to work, they might as well reduce their tax burden by making a move! The states losing the most residents lately are California and New York. Many people left for Florida, Tennessee, Texas, and other places with a 0 percent state income tax rate. Those states try to attract families and businesses through the lower cost of living and tax savings.

In California, where I live, there are proposals to raise the state income tax rate to as high as 16.6 percent for the higher income earners. If the highest federal tax rate moves from 37 percent to 39 percent, as is being proposed, then the highest earners living in California would be paying nearly 56 percent income tax on a portion of their income earned. As a result, when high income earners make a dollar, they get to keep less than half of their income, especially when factoring in social security, Medicare, and other taxes.

WHAT DO I TEACH MY KIDS ABOUT TAX LAWS?

While it's true nothing is certain except for death and taxes, taxes tend to be complicated and very inconsistent. The exact rules and amounts change all the time. Albert Einstein famously said, "The hardest thing in the world to understand is the income tax." In 2017, the US government passed the "Tax Cuts and Job Act," which lowered taxes for families and corporations and stimulated growth in the economy. However, nothing is permanent. There are talks now in 2021 to make major changes to tax rates and rules. So, you can't memorize rates or laws and think you're done. Teach your kids that it's important to keep up on the rules and readjust your financial planning and strategies accordingly. Your kids can take some comfort in knowing that tax planning is typically not a DIY endeavor.

Because the situation is complex and ever changing, there are tax specialists and professionals all throughout the country. Encourage your kids to seek professional guidance from fiduciaries and experts who can guide you in making decisions based on their situation as they grow up. No two people have the exact same situation, so it's impossible to make one-size-fits-all recommendations. What's best for each individual is personal and unique. As a result, kids don't need to learn all the ins and outs of current tax law, but they should understand that taxes are their biggest expense, tax laws exist and change, taxes come due every year, and they can benefit from professional financial guidance when they grow up.

Because taxes can take such a big bite out of your income, financial planning is important. General Cooley talks about the morality of tax planning. He says we are obligated to pay our taxes honestly and fairly, but there's no glory in overpaying from the money you've earned.

Moral tax planning is a fine line. I absolutely support paying for government services, including fire departments, police, and roads, etc. At the same time, I believe like General Cooley said, it's your right and duty to make financial decisions that can help you use financial planning to keep more of your hard-earned income for your family and for the charities and good people you take care of.

Making big financial decisions without planning for taxes represents an expensive mistake. For example, consider the investor who sells stock before holding it for one year and pays unnecessary capital gains taxes. If you buy an investment and hold on to it for at least twelve months instead, your gain goes from being considered short-term to long-term. Why does the difference matter? Long-term capital gains taxes are lower, at around 15 or 20 percent, whereas short-term capital gains get taxed like your regular income. Simply waiting to reach the twelve-month mark before selling your investment could be the difference between paying 15 percent and 35 percent in taxes!

If you make $300,000 a year, for example, and your new investment property appreciates $300,000 in a hot real estate market, and then you sell it within nine months, that $300,000 of gain in your investment just got added to your $300,000 of income— even though it wasn't income from a job. Now you owe income taxes on all $600,000 as if it came from an employer, when you could have just waited six months longer and paid a lower rate on the $300,000 appreciation. After twelve months, the government taxes the $300,000 separately as an investment gain, which in fact it really is. As a result, you could pay less than half the amount of taxes. So, knowing the rules can make a huge difference. I've seen people pay out a lot of money by making this mistake before.

Understanding taxes can help you make decisions that will save a significant amount of money down the road. For instance, I've sent emails to my clients on December 15 reminding them if they elect to take their bonus after the first of the year, they won't have to pay taxes on it for almost a year and a half. On the other hand, if they take it in December, they'll owe taxes in four months—

when tax day comes on April 15. Just waiting those two weeks gives you much more time to plan and invest. So, it's smart to ask if you can get your bonus on January 1 instead of December 31.

The value of understanding the basic ins and outs of tax laws— or at least recognizing that you don't and need help from an expert—is critical. Your kids may not care too much about it yet, but someday they will.

I remember a conversation with an NBA player client of ours when he had just signed his rookie contract as a teenager. He knew he wouldn't actually receive every dollar of his stated salary, but he hadn't realized how significant the taxes would be. The comparatively small amount remaining after taxes shocked him. It got worse when we explained we'd only covered federal income tax so far—on top of that amount, he'd have to pay state income tax to each of the twenty-one states he'd played basketball games in that rookie year.

His taxes were not simple, because his career represented the equivalent of running a business in twenty-one states. Even more confusingly, each state wants to count how much time you work there. If you're in New York for three days for a game against the Knicks, then the state wants to tax you for 3/365 of your income, because you spent the time there for the purpose of playing basketball. Earning a high income sounds great, but it can also be complicated and expensive—another reason your kids need to know that tax planning should be done thoughtfully and in advance of the due date.

No one had tricked this client; he'd just never had a clear explanation of his tax situation until he hired our team. Once we came on the scene, we wanted to make sure he and his family understood everything around their money decisions. Many athletes get $2 million contracts and think they can buy a $1.5 million house. In reality, though, they don't even get to keep half of their income.

Make sure your kids know that when they might someday earn $30 per hour, and work their 80 hours in two weeks, they will not be getting that full $2,400 deposited in their bank account from that paycheck. They will see the net pay after taxes and deductions are taken out. Don't wait for them to be unpleasantly surprised on the day of their first paycheck; be sure to explain the difference between gross and net income. One of my philosophies as a fiduciary financial advisor is to err on the side of overcommunicating with clients. I break everything down for them, so they're crystal clear about where they stand and what they need to do. Being transparent and honest gives people the real picture and helps them make better decisions—and the same philosophy could apply with you and your children. The more honesty and transparency, the better.

"One thing I try to have my clients do is pay their kids for working. If you can, have them file paperwork, learn basic bookkeeping and accounting skills, clean the office, or even attend tax and attorney meetings if they're older. This allows you as the parent(s) to receive a business tax deduction, helps the child(ren) learn about work and business, and allows the children to use that money for things they want/need to purchase!"

—BRADY SLACK, SENIOR TAX ADVISOR

WHAT DO I TEACH MY KIDS ABOUT TAX YEARS AND COMMON FORMS?

Tax obligations are typically measured on an annual calendar-year basis. Your kids can learn that you pay income tax for the calendar year on April 15 and have to file tax forms for yourself as well as for any businesses or investments you're involved in. Business tax returns may have different due dates than personal tax returns (many types of small businesses pay taxes on March 15), but they're all required to be filed formally each year. A business or self-employed person also typically pays estimated taxes four times a year. People in that situation should consult their professional advisor for guidance.

Teens should know they'll need to fill out tax forms when they get their first job. They'll fill out a W-4 to tell the employer how much in taxes to withhold from their paycheck, and at the end of the year, they'll get a W-2 summarizing their paychecks for the year from their employer.

Based on all the financial decisions and income you've made during the year, you'll owe a certain amount of taxes. Withholding taxes from your paycheck is a standard way to pay that amount in monthly installments, since most people living paycheck to paycheck would not be able to afford a lump-sum bill at the end of the year. If you're an employee, those installments get taken out of your paycheck. If you withhold nothing, you'll owe a larger lump sum in April.

Independent contractors fill out a W-9 and get a 1099 tax statement at the end of the year, and they usually pay quarterly estimated taxes instead of having automatic withholding from their paychecks. More and more young people these days are doing freelance work, which will often fall under the "1099 income" category. For example, if you are doing construction work, website or social media work, interior design consulting, or other freelancing work where people hire you for projects but not as a full-time employee, it's very likely you will be paid 1099 income. It's important for people in that situation to gather documentation on all the different deductible expenses you've made during the year, which your tax professionals can help you with. Helping your teenagers keep track of potentially deductible expenses will teach them about tax planning and also help them keep more of their hard-earned income. Common deductions for business owners, freelancers, and self-employed people include a home office, insurance, laptop computer, supplies, and work-related travel. These are good for kids to know, since some kids do run their own startup businesses, including lawn mowing, snow shoveling, photography, social media market-ing, or running their own YouTube channels. My friends Mike and Liz Ord have a son, Henry, who is very entrepreneurial. He is an outdoorsman and fisherman who turned his love of fishing into a few different small businesses, one of which he later sold to a customer out of Texas. What began with selling T-shirts, hats, and gear for fishermen turned into creating and molding customized fish bait (to match the colors and scents of the bait fish in the local ponds of his customers) to sell all over the country.

Besides the great entrepreneurial lessons and experiences Henry went through, he was able to take business-related deductions for expenses that included doing something he really enjoyed with his friends! Imagine your kids getting a little taste of entrepreneurship while also learning some things about how to navigate taxes and financial planning.

Various 1099 forms also summarize interest earned and investment income or losses for the year. An annual form called the K-1 lists the income distributions received from an investment you own or a partnership you're involved in.

When you file your taxes, the 1040 is the basic tax form. Many people use TurboTax or other DIY tax programs when they're first starting out, because it automates much of the filing process and allows people to do their own taxes. I still definitely recommend having a professional look over returns, though, to make sure you're not missing anything.

WHAT DO I TEACH MY KIDS ABOUT TAX REFUNDS?

People often celebrate getting a tax refund like they won a free prize. Yay, free money! What should we buy? Well, not so much. Please teach your kids not to celebrate getting a large tax refund. I want to be very clear: the perfect scenario is actually owing nothing on April 15—and getting zero refund.

Yes, I'm serious.

Your refund or tax bill due is effectively a measurement of how far off your tax prepayments and tax withholdings were. If you owe money at tax time, then you underpaid through your withholding or estimated payments, and now you have to make up the difference. A big refund means you gave the government way too much money the whole year, and now you're getting your own money back later—that's it. Had you planned better, you could have had more money to spend or invest during the year.

Theoretically, with each successive tax season, you should get better at planning and predicting what you owe. If you get a huge refund and your income is staying the same, withhold less. If you owe a lot at tax time, withhold more. That means it's good to revisit your withholding or your estimated tax payments (if you own your own business) at least once a year, after tax time, and figure out what you could do differently next time to prepay the actual right amount owed.

Too often, people get a refund, and they treat it like a free, unexpected bonus. It's not. They splurge for a new watch, an iPhone, a pricey vacation or even a car. They don't realize this money is not extra—it's their own money that they overpaid. Its size indicates they have no grasp on their actual budget and taxes due. Their numbers are off, and they need a plan. If you have trouble making one on your own, a fiduciary financial planner can help ensure you don't get a refund and don't owe anything extra.

DO TRY THIS AT HOME: FAMILY ACTIVITIES

Try the following with your kids to open up conversations about taxes.

The Ice Cream Lesson. Give your child a scoop or a big serving of ice cream. Then, take away one-third and eat it yourself—that amount represents taxes. You can also take a bite of everything they order and call it the "parent tax." Since I enjoy sampling different foods and desserts, I often use this teaching method with my five children. It's a funny and real way to teach kids of any age about the reality of taxes. (Sorry, kids! We are just trying to help you learn.)

The Pay Stub Reveal. Review a sample pay stub together in detail. Go through each line and explain what it means. Look at all the different categories of taxes and other deductions. Discuss the difference between the gross pay and net pay shown on the pay stub. Odds are your kids will be shocked at the amounts they see.

Review Receipts. Save a receipt—from a store, a restaurant, or another business—and walk through it with your kids line by line. Explain the cost of the item, the sales tax, the tip (if applicable), and so on. Ask them questions along the way to ensure they comprehend the exercise in an age-appropriate way, and be sure to answer their questions thoughtfully.

CHAPTER 5

———

LEARN TO EARN

"The money you make is a symbol of the value you create."

—IDOWU KOYENIKAN

One summer, my kids had an idea to make some money for themselves to save up for a day at Knott's Berry Farm. Their idea would cost some money up front (to buy inventory) that they didn't have, so they approached the Bank of Dad. After listening to their pitch, I decided it would be a good learning opportunity for them. At their request, I made an Amazon purchase of one hundred dollars' worth of red, white, and blue glow stick bracelets and necklaces that my three older kids wanted to sell during the upcoming July 4 community gathering. Going into the plan, they weren't sure whether they could turn a profit. It was a bit of a risk. To give them a greater incentive and sense of urgency to actually make some sales, I explained it's a big commitment to buy one hundred dollars' worth of inventory. If they didn't sell it, they'd still have to pay me back for that initial investment I was making. If they went to the July 4 festival at the park and got swept up only playing Frisbee, dancing to the live band, hanging out with their friends, and going to the booths and bounce houses, they probably wouldn't sell enough to break even on their costs. It was going to take a little work.

We arrived at the park just before sunset. I advised them that dusk meant it was "game time," because people would be inclined to buy their product when it was dark out and the sticks were glowing, not during the day. At first, they felt some reluctance and hesitation to get started. What if nobody wanted to buy them? That would be embarrassing. Plus, their friends were all keeping them distracted from their business opportunity. One was playing football and having fun with friends. Another worried his friends would see him trying to run a business and make fun of him, or that it would be embarrassing to approach strangers.

I huddled up the kids and reminded them while they owed me one hundred dollars, I thought they could actually make plenty of profits in a short amount of time if they put themselves out there and had a fun attitude about it. They could approach kids with their parents and say, "Look at these cool Fourth of July bracelets and necklaces that glow in the dark—don't you guys want some?" I encouraged them to follow through on their original plan and just see what happened. If they weren't having success after fifteen or thirty minutes, we could regroup and try a different plan.

As it turned out, not only did the plan work, but I also couldn't even find them when the fireworks started nearly forty-five minutes later because they were still out selling. They were mingling among thousands of people throughout the large park and grassy field, and my wife got worried that they were missing. I knew they'd come back, though. Their sales must've been going great, and I assumed that they were immersed in their business at the moment. When they rejoined us, they were so excited! It turned out they didn't have to worry about approaching people to sell after too long, because families sitting on their blankets from every direction actually waved them over to buy five or six items at a time for their family.

After the fireworks show, we went home and counted up all the money they earned. They paid me the one hundred dollars for the inventory plus five dollars of interest (the Bank of Dad needs to be paid for taking the risk) and found they'd made $260 of profit in less than forty-five minutes of work! They had a lot of fun in the process, too, because people were excited to engage in conversation and buy from them. They enjoyed the experience more than doing a chore like mowing the lawn or raking leaves. My son Sterling (eight years old at the time) mentioned how fun it was to see people get excited to put on their new glow-in-the-dark necklace or bracelet. The kids really enjoyed working with people directly. This offered our older three kids a great learning experience, and it didn't take away their enjoyment of the holiday—they had a blast.

The July 4 sales experiment also worked because it stemmed from their goals, not a lesson I tried to force on them. There were items they wanted to buy and activities they wanted to do during the summer that would cost a lot of money. I agreed to pay for some of the costs, but not everything. My wife and I told them they needed to figure out a way to make more money. **Just because you can afford to give your kids everything they want does not mean that you should.** Truthfully, sometimes I take some heat from my wife for insisting our kids do extra work or learn a tough lesson about money instead of just handing over the cash (or the goods, or the experience). But just like in this instance a few years back, our kids come away with more appreciation and an experience they can learn from. Their motivation to get what they wanted off their list drove them to get creative and put in the work. Our approach of paying for some but not all of their wants and wishes goes back to my overarching philosophy of helping them become smart, not spoiled, and the successful July 4 business shows the power of that philosophy.

> "My sixteen-year-old son has a part-time job where he works every day after school. He has his own checking account and his paycheck is directly deposited every payday. Earning his own money and monitoring his own bank account helps him be more independent than just always asking for money from Mom and Dad. He learns about the value of money and earns it through his own honest hard work. He is saving up to pay for his own used car, and now understands that money doesn't just grow on trees!"
>
> —VALERIE BALDOWSKI, WRITER

WHAT DO I TEACH MY KIDS ABOUT THE RESPONSIBILITY OF HAVING A BANK ACCOUNT?

By the age of fourteen, and certainly no later than sixteen, your child should have their own bank account and debit card. It's not a credit card, so they can only spend what they have in the account. Hopefully by the time they reach that age, you've helped them develop some good financial habits and an understanding of the guidelines for earning money to put in the account.

Making purchases with their own card tied to their own savings allows them to apply what you've taught them to real-world situations. When they ask if they can go to a birthday party, for example, you can agree with the caveat they buy the gift themselves. That's exactly what we do in our family. Of course, it's easier and more conflict-free to say yes to every party and simply buy everything to go along with it. However, taking the other route gives your kids experiences to help them learn to earn, to save, and to spend their own money. You can certainly put limits on spending, but mostly you want them to have concrete practice with making financially responsible decisions before they turn eighteen, leave home, and have no supervision or help. Besides your local bank, Greenlight is another company that offers a debit card program for kids, managed by parents. If you want to avoid common financial pitfalls, college is too late for your kids to open and use a bank account for the first time.

WHAT DO I TEACH MY KIDS ABOUT THE VALUE OF TIME AND MONEY?

I'll explain this concept with a story: a couple years ago, my kids wanted to participate in several gift exchanges at school and with their friends. The sheer number of gift exchanges and the associated costs started to feel ridiculous to me and my wife. We have five kids and were going to end up spending many times more money on their exchange gifts for parties than what we would on them for Christmas. We had to reset expectations and decided that after a certain amount, the kids would have to pay their own way for all these parties and gift exchanges.

My kids often do small jobs at my businesses, such as clerical or janitorial work at our main Pacific Capital office. I'm also the co-founder and co-owner of the Draft Sports Complex, where they earn ten dollars an hour working at the snack bar or at the front desk collecting the entrance fees during sports tournaments, giving people wristbands, and making change. All three of my older kids have worked at the Draft Sports Complex before. My son Pierce worked there on a Saturday for six hours and made sixty dollars. He donates 10 percent to our church, which left him fifty-four dollars. We encourage our kids to invest or save at least a third of what they earn, so in the end, he had about thirty-four dollars to spend.

Once he got paid, we went to the store so he could look around for his gift exchange idea for another party he wanted to attend. He got excited about an UNO Attack card game, but it was sixteen dollars plus tax.

"That's a lot, Pierce," I told him. "That's almost two hours' worth of work at the Draft Sports Complex." I asked him to think about the fact he could work for an entire two hours and then blow the income earned in just five minutes at Walmart.

"But Dad, the gift is basically my entrance into this fun party, and the party is two hours long. So, I'm trading two hours of work last Saturday for two hours of fun with my friends," he said.

Wow! I thought he'd made a great point. Then, he reminded me that he would also get a gift back that would have a value of at least ten dollars—meaning his personal net cost wouldn't be the full twenty bucks. In other words, he wasn't being impulsive. Pierce thought it through and understood the costs and benefits at play, and he made an informed decision for himself. Because of all the conversations we've had and money exercises we've done, at age thirteen, he was already thinking about the relationship between money and time as well as cost and value.

It's not easy to teach your kids to be smart instead of spoiled. It takes work and resilience. It's much easier for you to avoid the hassle of teaching and training them and instead just buy them what they're asking for. But your goal is to help them learn more about money than you were taught, and that will take a little effort up front. It will be worth the effort, I promise.

> *"Our family is in the farming industry, and all the kids and grandkids have to work on the farm for college money; it is not a given. Hard work and earning your own way are core values in our family that we expect everyone to develop. To this day, we call it a 'college farm' instead of a 'college fund.'"*
>
> —ANDY MUXLOW, CO-OWNER OF FAMILY TREE FARMS

WHAT DO I TEACH MY KIDS ABOUT THE DIFFERENCE BETWEEN EARNINGS AND INCOME?

Kids should understand earnings are your compensation for work. People receive money for the value of the work they do. **You can either be paid for your time or for your results.** When my children work at our sports facility, they're paid for their time. If they get a job at the movie theaters or Chick-fil-A, they will also be paid for their time. Work more hours, earn more money. For their household chores and projects, they're paid for results. When they sold glow sticks on July 4, they were also paid for the results, the outcome, no matter how much time it took them.

We generally use "earnings" to refer to active income, money you get from working and exchanging your time, but income more generally comes from many sources, including investments—not just from working. Teach your kids that you can build somewhat of a safety net if you create ways to earn income besides your job alone.

You can invest money you earned from your work, then generate passive income without having to putting in additional active work that requires your time. For instance, I don't work at the Draft Sports Complex. I invested a significant amount of money to help start it with a few business partners. Two of them run the business every day, so they get a higher percentage of ownership and profits. The situation works well for me, because I don't have extra time to go over and personally work there. I just get passive income every month from my investment in this business. Collecting rent on properties you invest in can also be a great source of passive income.

You can also earn income from stock dividends. At the time of this writing (2021), interest rates are lower than they've ever been in history. Banks literally pay you no income to keep your money in savings; current rates are around 0 or 0.1 percent. This situation is bad for savers and for people who are retired and living on their fixed-income investments each month. When sitting idle, your money loses value to inflation (discussed in detail in Chapter 1). On the other hand, if you own stocks or real estate that pay anywhere from 2 to 6 percent a year in dividends or rental income, then you keep your potential to grow the value of your money.

Teach your kids not to be afraid of investing. If they believe that investing and seeing investments fluctuate scares them, they will never learn how to achieve financial freedom and independence. You can show them the big trade-off and actual risks of not investing versus investing for the long term. Your kids will naturally believe it's safer to leave their money in the 0 percent interest bank account because the nominal value won't fluctuate up and down each day. However, if inflation is 3 percent and your savings earn nothing, then you're actually deciding to shrink your money by 3 percent every year. You're accepting and actually choosing a guaranteed loss of 3 percent per year instead of the potential to gain 7 or 10 percent per year. Plus, as an investor (in assets like stocks and rental real estate), while you patiently wait for the appreciation and growth, you can continue to earn dividends or rental income.

Please discuss the emotional side of making money decisions with your kids. I dedicated an entire chapter on "Feelings" as an obstacle to financial freedom in my book, *Stress-Free Money.* It's so important to make decisions based on facts, data, and logic, not emotional feelings and fear. Learning to gather data, look at the numbers, and choose accordingly lead to a stress-free relationship with money. Your kids can learn to decide what is a good potential investment and what the risks are without being paralyzed by fear. Not all investment and savings vehicles are equal payers of income. Similarly, not all jobs are equal payers. You could work at the Draft and earn ten bucks an hour, or you could go to the festival in the park and earn one hundred. Your kids may have talents or personalities that fit different types of opportunities. So, choose carefully where to give your time, attention, and effort. Look at all the options. Kids should not be all measured in the same way nor directed towards the same type of opportunities. Some kids would prefer that steady paycheck and predictable income, and that's great! Others will tend to lean more towards a job in sales. Either way, as they grow up and start their careers and families, encourage them to not rely solely on one source of income.

At Pacific Capital, we want our clients to have at least seven different sources of income before they retire. I often use the analogy of planting many seeds and having multiple trees that produce different kinds of fruits. Kids should understand that basic concept of cultivating a variety of income sources. You could tell them about the analogy of the brother and sister who were selling sunscreen at the beach on the tropical island. Every day that the sun was brightly shining, their sales were high, and they made a lot of money. However, being on a tropical island, there were many days that were full of pouring rain with zero sunlight to be found. If they only depended on the sunscreen sales, then half of the year would be days with no income…so they decided to begin to sell umbrellas and waterproof ponchos on the rainy days. With two income sources instead of one, they are now better prepared to "weather the storm."

> "My dad always taught me to buy from kids at lemonade stands or candy bar fundraisers, etc. The legacy continues with me and my wife teaching our children the same. Our oldest is seventeen, and all of our kids are doing entrepreneurial things around their passions and dreams. It's like they get to live many lives before they get out on their own—while still enjoying it and making the most of that one and only time they get to be kids."
>
> —RICHIE NORTON, MBA, AWARD-WINNING CEO, BESTSELLING AUTHOR OF *THE POWER OF STARTING SOMETHING STUPID*

BIDDING ON HOUSEHOLD CHORES

There are many productive ways to get kids thinking about how to earn money that help them learn the value of their work. I've taught our kids to look around, identify a need, figure out how to solve the need, and then negotiate the value of that solution. As I mentioned earlier, we don't give our kids a standard weekly allowance. Instead, they earn money each week based on the work they choose to do. For example, when they ask me what they can do to earn an extra ten or twenty bucks, I suggest they look around the house, see what needs to be done, and then make a proposal. They learn much more creativity, industriousness, and independence that way than if I just told them to go clean the toilets for ten dollars.

Here I am laying sod and doing yard work at eight years old. Check out my dad in the background watching me, hands on the hips.

My oldest daughter has gotten quite good at bidding on projects. A great example comes from my home office library that is a minefield of books. On average, I read about three books a week, more than 150 books a year. Even so, my waiting list of books I haven't yet read piles up faster than you can imagine. My home office has books stacked on the desk, on the ground, in the drawers, and sometimes new books arrive and land on the couch. It gets out of control. They're everywhere and it drives my wife crazy. She says I have too many. Do I really need to keep buying more? Don't I have enough? My response is the same: "We don't need fewer books; we just need more bookshelves."

At one point, when my office was completely out of hand, my daughter McKinley, who was fifteen at the time, pointed out what a mess the room was. She suggested helping me completely clean and organize it as a project to earn some extra money. She proposed to categorize each of the hundreds of books by subject, put them in different sections of my library, and make an effort to clean everything up. She said she'd find duplicate books to donate as well. McKinley estimated it would take three to four hours to do the project, which was an underestimate. Then she estimated the project to be worth forty dollars.

I agreed to her proposal, and she got to work. By the time she was done, she'd made an enormous difference. The office looked immaculate, the library spotless and organized. My books were categorized and easy to find. Looking at the results and the extra hours spent beyond her initial estimate, I told her she'd done a job worth closer to eighty dollars, so I'd pay her more than we'd agreed upon because she'd done so well. Of course, she was pleased—and motivated to find more ways to provide value around our house that could result in some extra income.

WHAT CAN I TEACH MY KIDS ABOUT *THEIR* INCOME OPPORTUNITIES?

With the right systems in place, kids learn the opportunities for earning money are as endless as their creativity. Even very young kids can get creative about creating value and contributing to your family, and your older kids can earn a substantial income while still in high school.

For instance, one fall, my friend Brett Shield's kids got hooked on snow cones. There were a number of snow cone businesses set up in the neighborhood, and they constantly went with their buddies to buy them. They kept hitting up their dad for another five or ten dollars, until he'd finally had enough. He said if they wanted to keep making purchases, they'd have to figure out a source of income.

The kids are in their early- and midteens, and they came up with a solution that goes above and beyond the cost of a snow cone. In the winter, they shovel snow, and in the summer, they maintain yards. Brett helped them make flyers. Once they started making a little money, he helped them invest in better equipment. They now have a full-fledged small business and make thousands of dollars a week. They're saving for their own cars already, and it all happened because their dad said no. Instead of paying for their every whim, he forced them to get creative.

Brett's approach shows the importance of empowering rather than enabling. When kids own their efforts, they shine. I've learned the importance of empowerment having been a Boy Scout leader for nearly eighteen years. Troops of young people thrive when adults ask what kids think they should do, rather than telling them what to do. I ask which activities, adventures, and lessons they'd like to plan for the next two months rather than telling them to sit down and listen to my agenda for them. The same concept applies to kids' options for earning money— they come up with the goal and then figure out how to meet it.

> *"If you don't find a way to make money while you sleep, you will work until you die."*
>
> —WARREN BUFFETT

WHAT DO I TEACH MY KIDS ABOUT FINDING A CAREER?

Parents can play a huge, positive role in helping their kids find a career that they love, that they're good at, and that will support them to be financially independent someday. In helping your child explore careers, it's important to look at their unique abilities, traits, and preferences. Steer them toward ways to earn income that fit those skills and interests, rather than trying to make them fit a career you think is most important or prestigious.

If you try to force your child into a box, it tends to backfire. Many parents say, "This is how I made money; therefore, it's also how you need to make money"—but of course, your kids are different from you. They often don't know any better, though, so they assume if their dad is a dentist or an accountant, they should be a dentist or an accountant. Or if their mom is a lawyer or real estate agent, they should be a lawyer or real estate agent. It's rare for them to learn to look for roles in their own unique wheelhouse.

I am a co-owner of the company called My First Sale (www. myfirstsale.com) with partners and co-founders Scott Donnell and Travis Adams. Our business exists to help young kids learn how to make money and manage money well. We want to help them tap into their talents and passions and learn to earn money while doing things they enjoy and have unique abilities in. We are doing virtual business fairs all throughout the country for kids who have created their own businesses. Given the chance, kids will blow you away. And we know that when a young person sells something they made with their own hands to someone else who loves it, they have confidence for life. Soon, our app will be done, and we envision that as something that impacts kids globally. We will have certifications around financial literacy, a digital wallet for kids, and the ability to manage and spend their money wisely. We love to see kids learn and develop money and business skills that will give them such confidence and a foundation for their future.

Remind your kids they shouldn't despise what they do to earn money. Being miserable at work for five days a week to have two weekend days of freedom is no way to live life. That situation is miserable. We all spend a good portion of our lives working to pay our bills, so it's important to enjoy what we do. Show your kids that if they're creative and find ways to make money doing what they enjoy, they'll be so much happier than if they have to drag themselves out of bed to get to a job they hate doing, and remember that each of your children will do this differently.

PARENT TIP

What *is* success, anyway? That's a big question. I teach my kids to be successful by finding what they like to do, developing the skill to be good at it, and ensuring that skill is valuable enough that others will pay them for it. To be financially independent in a successful way, they must have all three elements. Having only one or two won't work.

My cousin went to business school because his dad was a high-profile tax partner at a large firm in downtown Los Angeles. He earned his degree in accounting like his dad, but later realized he hated it. It wasn't fun at all. Now, he's a longhaired surfer, videographer, and photographer and is producing cool videos and commercials for big-time companies. He says he's found what he was meant to do. It's not what his dad had in mind, but he loves it, is good at it, and gets paid for it. He's had jobs doing commercials for major car companies and has even traveled the world to get international surfing footage for some of the jobs he's had. It checks all the boxes of earning money while doing something he loves, so he's successful.

Teach your kids not to measure success solely by the amount of money they make. That narrow metric represents a real problem in our society. Money is not a scoreboard of comparison. Career success needs to check all three boxes. With that understanding, your kids will know what true success looks like and how to measure it. This will liberate your kids to know that they don't work in the same field doing the same things as you have done. Your kids can be free to explore what gets them excited. They'll also understand that the world largely pays you what it thinks your work is worth, and they'll be able to use that in the future to determine what makes a hobby versus a career.

Start talking to your kids about career options, industries, and income no later than fifth grade. By that time, they already know what they like and dislike. They have favorite subjects that come naturally and ones they dread. Even before that age, you can still encourage activities and skill building they feel drawn toward. My five-year-old son, Beckham, for instance, loves building and hands-on activities, so we give him similar games and opportunities in those domains. From very early on, he was building towers and castles with Lego toys and even putting together 200- and 300-piece puzzles. We regularly buy small building kits for him to work on—little gadgets and remote-control cars to put together. For more specific ideas and companies that have STEM building kits for kids, refer to resources at www.pacificcapital.com/smartnotspoiled.

My oldest son, Pierce, is also a hands-on person. He's very different from me in that he's good at taking things apart and putting them together and that doesn't come natural to me at all. He's a builder and engineer who loves to use his hands and see how things work. I know there's no way he could enjoy doing what I do, because my business is all conceptual—communication, vision, strategy, and planning. I don't need to physically touch things to make them happen in my job. We've discussed careers that might appeal to him, including real estate development, engineering, and medicine. Those fields involve using your hands, seeing how systems work on the inside, building, creating, and fixing.

For Christmas or his birthday, we give him presents that are robotic or remote-control items he gets to build from scratch. Like his little brother Beckham, Pierce always loved Lego and other toys that allow him to create structures. We help him pursue and foster those interests, knowing if he develops skills aligned with his passions, he's more likely to land in a financially sustainable career he loves.

I understand the temptation to want your child to follow in your footsteps or even to take over a family business you have. There's a desire for that legacy to continue on. My warning would be to not try to force that to happen. Sometimes, you can develop roles within such a business that suit your child's interests and abilities, if they want to go in that direction. I often say the industry is less important than the mission and the fit, if the child has the inclination. However, there's no point in trying to fit a round peg into a square hole.

Plus, it's worth considering that if multiple siblings or one child of multiple children take over a family business, the situation could get messy. It's common for conflicts to arise around who works more or less, who takes more or less time off, and how much money everyone makes. I've seen many clients handle their family business succession situations differently over the years; some turned out well and others resulted in fractured family relationships. Sometimes your child simply isn't the best person to take over the enterprise you've built. At least it needs to be thoughtfully considered and planned out if that is the route your kids want to take.

When it comes to tying your kids' future income expectations to their career field, think of this Elon Musk tweet, "You are paid in direct proportion to the difficulty of the problems you solve." So, if they want to earn more money, they need to solve bigger problems—that's the key. That explains why a brain surgeon earns more money than a street sweeper. More people can step in and do street sweeping than brain surgery. Kids should understand this concept so they can see why salaries and incomes aren't random.

"From a young age our daughter Abby, now 17, has had career aspirations in the field of early childhood development. We're fortunate in that we live in a small community neighborhood in north coastal San Diego County filled with families, many of whom have small children and active parents. As you can imagine, Abby is in high demand for babysitting and even carries her business cards with her to neighborhood gatherings and socials.

"Early in her babysitting career, she was confronted with having to answer the awkward question, 'What do we owe you?' or 'What do you charge?' This can be an intimidating question for a teenager to address with an adult. To help her maneuver through this challenge, we discussed the importance of knowing your value. We talked about there being two parts to the equation: the amount that the customer, in this case the parents, was happy to pay for exceptional service, and the amount Abby needed to feel both valued and eager to provide the service again at the same rate in the future.

"To help Abby determine the first part, we showed her how to check the rates in our community using online apps like Nextdoor. She felt those rates were fair, but she also realized she could increase her value by adding certifications such as first aid, CPR, etc.—which she did. She now enjoys a steady income at fair, up-front, and agreed-upon rates while getting tons of experience in a field she loves."

—BEN NEVEJANS, PRESIDENT AT LIFEPRO

WHAT DO I TEACH MY KIDS ABOUT PLAYING TO THEIR STRENGTHS?

If you're trying to help an older child identify their strengths and potential career paths, I'd recommend a Kolbe Student Aptitude assessment for kids and the Clifton StrengthsFinder (more resources listed on www.pacificcapital.com/smartnotspoiled). These assessments are aimed at helping children ages 11–17 discover a great deal about how they make decisions, their instincts, how to communicate, and the situations in which they're most likely to excel. As an adult, you can also take the Kolbe A Index and the StrengthsFinder by Gallup along with them, helping you learn more about yourselves and each other.

As a business owner myself, I acutely understand the importance of playing to strengths and finding a good career fit. I want all of my team members at work to be fully energized and loving what they do. We make sure every role and task fits their unique abilities. That way, they are energized and fully engaged in their work. And when they go home, they're not drained from a long and tedious day. They leave work feeling pumped up and excited about what they worked on.

Once a month, we have a team meeting facilitated by a Kolbe- and Clifton-certified coach. We talk through projects that were a great success and discuss challenges or bottlenecks in the business. People share what parts of their job they liked and didn't like in the last month. We write the challenges up on the board in our conference room, the tasks that individuals dreading working on, and then ask the entire group if anyone else actually enjoys that activity and would gladly take it off the plate of a coworker. For instance, some people actually love filling out client data forms for new accounts and the sense of accomplishment from that kind of organizational task, while others may dread all that detailed information. That's an easy switch if you are a leader who is paying attention to your people. From there, we can reshuffle responsibilities to get the best fit. As a result, the level of energy and enthusiasm goes up and people are doing more of what they enjoy doing and less of what they dread.

The same general principle applies to your kids. They need to know they can make money and like what they do. I don't think people should have to dread workdays or school days. In my family, I emphasize uncovering our strengths and interests and figuring out how to enjoy what we're doing. **At MyFirstSale. com, we currently show nearly 200 small business ideas for kids, so they have a menu from which to choose ideas that fit their interests**. Work doesn't always have to be a struggle; it's important to enjoy your own life journey.

Part of enjoying the journey means choosing the right fit for how you will earn money throughout your life. Not just the right fit for what you will do every day at work, but with whom you will spend your time doing it. Teach your kids that job interviews often aren't so much about getting a particular job as vetting your future boss. The people you work around are at least as important as the work you'll be doing. Who you work with every day will majorly impact your life. The interpersonal fit with your supervisor and coworkers is sometimes more important than the specific role you fill. Your kids may not ever consider that as they are typically only focused on the name and reputation of the company and the money they will earn.

In fact, there's conventional wisdom that you never quit your job, you only quit your boss. Employees often leave not because of the work but because of the people. As your kids enter the workforce, if they have multiple job opportunities that pay similar amounts, encourage them to pay attention to the people they'll be working with and choose the best fit. It's not just about the money—there's more to your work and career than just the dollars on the paycheck. Help your kids learn to make choices that play to their skillset strengths and personality.

> *"The best way to teach your kids about money is through hard work. Work ethic by far will be the most important characteristic in the future for our kids for their ability to make a living. In an era and generation of entitlement, those who work hard will be easily recognized in the future.*
>
> *"Regarding work ethic, I always try to look for ways to put my kids in difficult or tough situations. Most millionaires I know have been beat up financially a few times. They didn't give up. They kept getting up when they were knocked down. Don't bail your kids out; see how they react, and guide them. The world's a scary place, and you won't always be around to help them through.*
>
> *"For us, my wife, Amy, and I helped our kids set up bank accounts at young ages. When summer starts, they wake up at 5:30 a.m. six days a week and pick fruit on the farm. Then, they take that fruit to the fruit stand at 9 a.m. They work every day until 5 p.m., and then they start over the next day. They get to keep the proceeds of the sales. I know that not everyone lives on a farm, but we can all find ways to teach our kids to be more responsible and work hard. Expect more, and they will do more!"*
>
> —DANIEL JACKSON, EIGHTH-GENERATION FARMER, CO-OWNER OF FAMILY TREE FARMS

Don't Forget the Basics. Monopoly is a classic game that can be an excellent tool to help talk about the concepts of handling money. When your child "earns" money from rent on a property, talk to them about what it would be like if they owned all three. What if they had hotels instead of houses? If they want to have that kind of investment income in real life, brainstorm some ways they could make their passion and that dream a reality. It's never too early to set goals and talk about what is possible.

See a Need, Fill a Need. Swap allowance for "see a need, fill a need," in which your kids can search on their own for what needs to be done, then pitch you a job and a cost for their work. Do they want to scrub/mop/dust? How much do they think it is worth? Are they over- or undervaluing the work? Thinking in this way helps them build their entrepreneurial/growth mindset and encourages them to build skills they'll utilize later on. It also takes the burden off of you as the parents to do their thinking for them. Develop their ability to be resourceful and take initiative! You might consider overpaying them when they source the idea for work around your house as that will get them excited to keep it going!

Try MyFirstSale.com. MyFirstSale.com is our platform that teaches kids how to make and manage money, and I'm proud to be a co-owner alongside Scott Donnell and Travis Adams. Here, we teach kids how to discover what they're interested in, give them ideas and inspiration (150+ business ideas to try!), and offer tools to start and market their own businesses. True to our mission of empowering kids, the CEO of MyFirstSale.com is Abbey Richter, who is sixteen. The site includes a shop, allowing parents or any visitors to browse the selection of unique, kid-created items. Whether your child is a budding entrepreneur already or is ready to give it their first shot, they'll find resources, support, and community at MyFirstSale.com. As Dan Sullivan says, "Talented young people that go on to do great things in the world almost always have a support system around them encouraging them."

CHAPTER 6

———

PROTECT WHO AND WHAT YOU CARE ABOUT

"Remember: when disaster strikes, the time to prepare has passed."

—STEVEN CYROS

In my experience, many adults don't totally understand insurance—which means your kids definitely won't unless you break it down for them. Do your kids realize, for instance, that the cost of driving a car is much more than just paying for gas? They should—and you have an opportunity to teach them!

WHAT DO I TEACH MY KIDS ABOUT WHY WE NEED INSURANCE?

Your child likely understands that not everything goes as planned in life. Reinforce this when explaining the purpose of insurance to them. Its purpose, of course, is to protect you from unexpected life situations when (not if) they occur. Insurance kicks in when you face an unforeseen expense as the result of some kind of accident, malfunction, or emergency. Maybe a water heater pipe breaks while you're on vacation, for example, and floods your entire house. I'm sure your kids have seen the commercials from State Farm or Allstate showing all kinds of random emergency disasters.

Dealing with insurance companies isn't always easy either. I've been a homeowner for sixteen years and have never made a claim on my home insurance policy, which has a high premium. I recently received a letter informing me that the carrier canceled mine because we live in an area that is near hills that could potentially catch on fire (though we've lived in the same home for well over a decade and the hills aren't new). Also, our trampoline isn't nailed into the ground, which they suddenly deem dangerous and uninsurable. Unfortunately, when you make claims on insurance, companies sometimes find a way not to pay. Still, you need to keep yourself covered and protected.

There are so many different types of insurance. Kids can learn to appreciate being careful and safe when they are told the cost of health, car, home, renter's, life, disability, and long-term care insurance, as well as why those policies are necessary and important. Knowing that everyone's actions in the family have consequences will teach them to be smart, not spoiled.

"Life insurance is not something that my family talked about growing up. However, through a tragic turn of events for a close friend of mine in my early adulthood I learned about the necessity of it. My friend and her husband, a helicopter crew chief in the United States Marine Corps, were both in their early thirties with four children ranging in age from seven months to six and a half years. After spending many weeks and months apart due to his military service, they decided that he would "ground" himself from flying for a few months in order to spend some quality time with his young family. One morning in May of 1993, he took an unplanned quick flight to assist on a helicopter repair and died in a crash.

"Overnight my friend found herself widowed with four young children. Thankfully, in addition to the $100,000 service members' life insurance benefit, my friend and her husband had the forethought after the birth of their last child to take out a personal life insurance policy on the husband with a substantial death benefit. It was because of this that my friend was able to raise her four children as a single, stay-at-home mother. Without the benefits that life insurance afforded my friend's family, all of their lives most likely would have been horribly different in their outcome. Her kids, now grown and with successful careers, know firsthand the value of life insurance. I have also used this experience to talk to my kids, friends, and parents about it, as well. Any opportunity I have to share her story, I do."

—HEATHER ULZ, CEO OF LIFEPRO

WHAT DO I TEACH MY KIDS ABOUT HEALTH INSURANCE?

Your children have certainly had the chance to visit a doctor's office in their young life. Have they ever wondered how much that doctor or hospital visit cost and who paid for it? Healthcare in America has become increasingly expensive, and the topic of health insurance coverage and costs inspires many strong opinions. Teach your kids that health insurance applies to both expected and unexpected healthcare expenses—including routine visits, medications, emergency stays, and serious surgeries—and can really get expensive when health issues or emergencies arise.

WHAT DO I TEACH MY KIDS ABOUT THE DIFFERENCE BETWEEN HOMEOWNERS AND RENTERS INSURANCE?

When your child moves out on their own, they'll need to consider renters insurance. When they grow into adulthood, they'll need to understand homeowners insurance. Here's how you can explain the basics: homeowners insurance covers unexpected, expensive events that damage or destroy your home, such as floods, theft, fires, etc. Renters insurance protects your belongings if you are renting a property.

The bottom line? When they go to college and rent their first apartment on their own, they would be wise to have a policy. Having coverage will protect them in case of emergency.

Here's an example of why: when my wife and I were dating, she was nineteen and sharing a rental house with friends up near our college campus. She and her roommates each left the area of our college town and went home to visit their parents during

Christmas break, and when they returned to the rental house, they found someone had broken in and stolen many of their belongings. Fortunately, she had renters insurance and was able to replace some of her stolen items, including her snowboard and boots, clothes, schoolbooks, and jewelry.

Sharing real-life examples like this—or your own of when you needed insurance—will help reinforce its value to your kids.

WHAT DO I TEACH MY KIDS ABOUT LIFE INSURANCE?

Nobody likes to talk about death. I get it. It's not a fun topic to think about. But this life insurance conversation is not one to skip.

Life insurance gives families a sense of security that they will continue to have financial stability if someone dies and their income goes away. By having such a policy, a tragic, untimely death will not also bring about material insecurity at the worst possible time. Parents who buy such policies get peace of mind that their families would be okay without them. Buying appropriate insurance coverage represents an act of love in a family. The surviving members will be taken care of, without having to worry about covering the mortgage or other expenses. Failing to have a policy is honestly selfish and irresponsible.

Life insurance involves paying money while you're alive so that when you die, a much larger, tax-free amount will go to your family than if you'd simply put the cost of your insurance policy into a bank savings account instead. You can decide the term of your life insurance policy—it could last for a specific period of time and then expire, or it could last your entire life. The health-ier and younger you are, the cheaper it is to buy, because you're less likely to die soon. A seventy-three-year-old smoker with health issues, on the other hand, would face a high premium, because they're statistically more likely to die in the near future.

Here's another example you can use to explain why this is such an important topic. One of my friends died recently of a sudden, entirely unexpected brain aneurysm at age forty. He was actually watching the Dodgers in the World Series on TV with two of his young kids, when he said he had a headache and needed to lie down. He stood up and fell straight to the ground, and he was gone in an instant. He left behind a wife and four kids. Despite me talking to him about life insurance multiple times, he just procrastinated taking the first steps and never got his policy set up. His wife had always been a stay-at-home mom and was less familiar with their family finances. After his death, she suddenly had four little kids to support and a mortgage to pay, with no income, which is a terrible situation for a widow.

> *"There's no harm in hoping for the best as long as you're prepared for the worst."*
>
> —STEPHEN KING

WHAT DO I TEACH MY KIDS ABOUT DISABILITY INSURANCE?

Just like death can be tough to talk about, so can disability. But again, it's part of the overall financial toolbox you can give your kids before they leave the nest. Here's how to start explaining at a high level: disability insurance covers the earnings you're missing out on due to disability. For example, imagine you work as a dentist. You're playing football on Thanksgiving Day and badly break your hand. Your hands are essential to your work, but now you're out of commission for eight months while your injury heals. If you can't work on patients in your dental practice, you won't get paid. In that situation, your disability insurance benefit payments would kick in, because you became disabled in a way that temporarily affects how you earn your income. Depending on your policy, it will replace all or a portion of the income you would be earning if not for your injury.

The intent of such insurance is to ensure you can meet your expenses if you become disabled and cannot work. If you want occupational disability insurance specific to your job, it will pay more when you are injured and also cost more in premiums. If the insurance policy is not specific to your occupation, then it will not pay out if you could still work in another field to earn some money. Maybe you couldn't be a dentist, but you could still deliver mail, for instance. Keep in mind whether your policy covers disability that prevents you from doing your current job or only pays if you are completely unemployable. If you went to medical school and become disabled in a way that prevented you from working as a doctor, then you'd want to make sure your specific job's income was covered. Otherwise, the insurance company could say it doesn't have to pay because you could still go work at McDonald's.

Unfortunately, some people game the system and are dishonest about the real nature of their conditions. They may or may not still actually be injured and unable to work, but they keep collecting money. When you discuss insurance with your kids, you can also talk about ensuring they are honest with insurance companies…insurance fraud could lead to more than just fines and penalties, but all the way up to prison sentences.

WHAT DO I TEACH MY KIDS ABOUT LONG-TERM CARE INSURANCE?

Long-term care insurance provides coverage when you need medical care for an extended period of time. It's usually used by people over age seventy who have an injury or illness. If they get out of the hospital and need an in-home caregiver, or actually have to move into a nursing home, the policy helps cover many if not all of those costs.

About two-thirds of adults will eventually have long-term care expenses because people are living so much longer these days. Medical advances are keeping people alive, but at some point, the elderly can no longer do everything on their own. Without insurance, long-term care can be extremely expensive and drive people into poverty. Twenty-four-hour care in California can cost as much as $350 per day, which would be close to $130,000 for a full year.

If you get sick or badly injured and don't have a policy already in place, then you have to pay the full cost of your care expenses. On the other hand, if you start a policy when you're healthy in your fifties or sixties, then you could end up paying something like ten or fifteen cents on the dollar for future care. So, such policies make a lot of sense, no matter if you can afford to pay the expenses out of pocket or not. Kids won't need long-term care insurance any time soon, but it's good for them to know what it is and that they might want it when they get older. They also might consider the future healthcare costs to take care of you, their parents!

DO TRY THIS AT HOME: FAMILY ACTIVITIES

Use Play Money. Gather a pile of board game money and put it on the dining room table. Explain what could happen if there is an emergency, showing examples of how much repairs, medical bills, or other losses can cost. When you're done, show a few examples of you putting a small amount together in a pile with an insurance company that already has a pile of money together. Then give an example of one family having an emergency and how the money comes out of that insurance pile that is shared with all the different families plus the insurance company...and explain why it's smart to pool your risk together with others.

Don't Sit, Stimulate Their Brains. Instead of just pooling play money alone, role-play an actual emergency. For example, if there's a fire, where will you and the kids go? What should they do? Walk through the whole drill. When you're done with the safety pieces, talk about what's next—including, of course, the financial relief of having insurance and some 'what if' scenarios if you didn't. This double whammy will help teach safety and money skills.

CHAPTER 7

———

GIVE GENEROUSLY

"We make a living by what we get. We make a life by what we give."

—WINSTON CHURCHILL

When I was growing up, my family frequently did service projects together. My parents and grandparents strongly believed in giving and taught me that money is not solely to be kept for ourselves, but it's for sharing and helping people in need. They encouraged me from a young age always to donate at least 10 percent of what I earned to church and other charities. I've done so my entire life, and now my kids have learned the same lessons from me and my wife.

My parents were respectably middle class, but not wealthy. We lived in a safe neighborhood and weren't poor, but we didn't go on fancy vacations or go out to eat at restaurants very often. Still, my parents demonstrated you don't have to be a millionaire to behave generously or to instill good values in your children.

We didn't travel the world as a family, but I learned a tremendous amount about life and being a good community member through my involvement in the Boy Scouts of America. We did service weekly. Once, when I was around thirteen years old, I signed up to volunteer with the Special Olympics in Los Angeles and stayed in the dorms for a week with the athletes when they came to UCLA to compete. Volunteers like us picked our sport of interest to serve in, and I picked basketball, helping coach wheelchair basketball for a Special Olympics team for the whole week. The experience was life-changing. I grew so close to these athletes who were quite different from me.

I look back on my volunteer work through the Boy Scouts and can see those moments that taught me how good it feels to be a giver. I felt motivated to become financially successful, because I knew the more I earned, the bigger impact I could make to help people in need. You can make a significant difference by giving no matter your wealth, but my giving experiences as a kid fostered my ambition to contribute as much as possible.

As a result, a few years ago, I brought my kids to participate in the Special Olympics when it came to Southern California. It felt like my childhood coming full circle. My two oldest kids volunteered as track-and-field coaches at the high school by our house for a regional Special Olympics event, and watching them serve there brought back all my positive memories of doing the same work.

Giving is one of the essential principles for kids to understand, because financial success includes living with purpose, meaning, and significance. Accumulating a bunch of money without a goal serves no positive purpose, and in the end, you can't take it with you anyway. Having money in and of itself is not the purpose of your existence. Life comes down to the quality of your relationships and not to how much money is in your bank accounts. The more you give, the more you receive. Kids can learn good financial values at a young age that will stay with them for a lifetime. It starts with you.

> *"No one has ever become poor by giving."*
>
> —ANNE FRANK

WHAT DO I TEACH MY KIDS ABOUT LIVING IN ABUNDANCE?

You obviously care about your child's future...which is why

you're reading this book. And as you already know, a healthy and positive future involves much more than just money.

Children who grow into giving adults contribute so much more to the world during their lives—not only through giving their money, but also their time, resources, service, and generosity. Learning to give instills a mindset of abundance rather than scarcity. This positive mindset unleashes so much potential for good outcomes and growth. Isn't this what you want to help create for your children? You can give them opportunities to connect with others while teaching them to be caring and giving individuals. Without that intentional effort, your kids may instead lean towards entitlement and selfishness—whether on a team, in a group at school, or once they're out working in the real world—and with that mindset and attitude, they won't go far in life.

Remember: money doesn't make you who you are; it magnifies who you are. It amplifies the traits and character that is already inside you. The more you give, the more you will receive in the long run. Giving money and service creates an abundance mindset. When your children give their money and time to a cause they care about, they learn that life is not all about them. The world is a big place, and you can teach them to make an impact even at a very young age. If your kids learn to hold everything back for themselves, they learn there isn't enough available to share with others. That limited worldview solidifies scarcity and fear in your kids' minds.

By contrast, giving freely of your money and time actually creates more abundance—more time and money—because you don't see it as so hard to get that you're afraid to lose it. Training your children to see the world through the lens of abundance, opportunity, connecting, and compassion is so much healthier than teaching them to focus on scarcity, hoarding, selfishness, competition, and limitations. Their mindset around giving will affect much more than just their financial lives as they grow up.

In general, I teach my kids: "See a need, fill a need." We almost never pass by homeless people or anyone who looks like they need help without offering something. If I get complacent or distracted and don't see it, my kids will tell me when they see someone in need of help. I'll ask my kids what they think we should do. One time, they saw a mother and daughter with a sign saying they were hungry, so we took the mother and daughter duo next door to Chipotle to get them something to eat. Our youngest kids talked about how happy the mom looked when she got her food. We make those gestures regularly, to the point the practice of giving has become ingrained in our family. My kids now look for those opportunities.

We also train our kids to give at least 10 percent to charity when they earn money. Doing so is part of our faith, so they've grown accustomed to the practice from their earliest days of receiving money without complaint. It's easiest to foster a giving habit if you start when kids are young, rather than introducing it later. If they know from their first ten dollars that they give 10 percent, save and invest 40 percent, and can spend 50 percent, then they'll keep applying a similar mindset to their budgeting and giving as they get older and the amounts get bigger.

Giving helps teach kids not to get attached to money and

material belongings. I'm a Christian, and I know people often misquote scripture as "Money is the root of all evil," but the scripture verse actually says, "The love of money is the root of all evil." I strongly believe money does so much good if it's in the right hands. The giving part takes away the love of money and the lust of that greedy selfishness. With a bit of intentional hands-on teaching, your kids learn to think far beyond themselves and their own wants.

> "Our focus today is making sure our kids turn out to be incredible people. They need to find causes they're passionate about and find ways to make the world a better place. Charitable giving is a core value for our family. We involve our children in many ways as we give to charities, including having different charities give presentations to our family. It's a great experience for our three young children to participate and then help us decide as a family where we will give our time and money. This involves our kids in the giving process and helps them be more vested in the cause."
>
> —CASEY (PRESIDENT OF VISIBLE SUPPLY CHAIN MANAGEMENT) AND ANGELA ADAMS (HIGHLY ACCOMPLISHED AND SUCCESSFUL ATTORNEY)

WHAT DO I TEACH MY KIDS ABOUT THE REWARDS OF GIVING?

My family has a Christmas tradition of giving to families in need. We shop with the kids and make the Christmas deliveries together. Sometimes we do it anonymously and other times we visit with the families in need to give them their gifts. It's not always during the holidays. Once during the back-to-school season, one of my kids' friends had multiple stressors at home:

their dad was battling stage 4 cancer, and their mom had just been laid off. We decided to get enough basic supplies for our kids but fewer extras, and we spent the savings on school supplies for the children in this family. We dropped everything off at their house, and each of our five kids gave them a backpack and a bag full of things for the new school year. It was a meaningful experience for us to see the joy on their faces. Their mom cried and told us how much it meant to them that their kids could start the school year out on a positive note, despite all the troubles at home.

The Christmas tradition started with my service as a volunteer church missionary. I lived in Lithuania, Latvia, Estonia, and Belarus for two years in the late nineties. Missionaries don't get paid; they pay their own way. During my two years in Eastern Europe, I met people who had almost nothing but still felt deeply grateful for what they did have. The experience made a lasting impression on me and motivated me to ensure my kids would someday be smart, not spoiled, about all the abundance of growing up in the USA. I quickly realized how much we had to be grateful for back home. As a father of five, I don't want to load up under the Christmas tree every year to the point they develop an entitlement attitude.

Also, when I was a kid, my parents sometimes encouraged us to sacrifice a few of our own gifts, rewrap them, and give them to a family that my parents knew was struggling financially. As I work to provide for my own family, it's also very important to me to keep paying that good fortune forward to those around us.

A few years ago, I took my kids to the settlement house, where people in poverty go to get a Christmas dinner, including ham, sides, and other groceries. We donated money and toys, and then we went for three hours as a family after church to help wrap and pass out gifts to the children in line. My kids helped people fill up their grocery carts with food and wrapped gifts and then unload the items into their cars. What a great experience to share together for hundreds of families in need. It changes our entire view of the holidays when we incorporate these activities.

> *"We've taught our children to give money to charity and donate to our church since they were younger. We always direct some of our donations to local causes, and I always let the kids pick which charities they want to give it to. Also, these little philanthropic league and charity groups they volunteer with that are often seen as résumé builders actually really get them in touch with charitable causes in our local community."*
>
> —MIKE ORD, PRESIDENT OF COMMERCIAL REAL ESTATE BROKERAGE

SERVICE VACATIONS

I personally love tropical vacations, so we often go somewhere tropical as a family. We went to the Bahamas a couple of years ago, and my wife suggested that instead of just doing fun excursions and lounging around the resort, we should engage the kids in some community service while visiting the island. So, on the second day of the trip, we went to an orphanage, filled out a lot of paperwork before being allowed to go, and spent the day volunteering there. We read to kids, played board games with them, and helped out for six or seven hours. The taxi driver who drove us from the resort was so perplexed that we'd spend money and time to go to an orphanage during our family vacation. He wasn't used to seeing Americans behave that way, he said.

By the fourth or fifth day of the vacation, our kids already missed the children at the orphanage and wanted to go back. When I asked how they wanted to spend their last day of the trip, most of them wanted to return to the orphanage and say goodbye to their new friends. Experiences like this help kids (and adults) become more compassionate, well-rounded people—and service becomes a more natural part of who they are.

In another instance a few years ago, we stayed at a resort in Jamaica as a family. At a bakery there, we met a Jamaican chef named Trinika. Trinika was working at the bakery every day of our trip. She was so nice and friendly and seemed to like our family every time we came to order food from her. I kept asking her why she didn't go outside after work and swim on these nice, sunny days; she made up all kinds of excuses, but we eventually learned it was actually because she didn't know how to swim. She was working at a beautiful resort with pools and beaches everywhere, but she couldn't enjoy the water. It terrified her. I talked to my kids about how they took their swimming skills for granted, and how this woman couldn't afford lessons. Then, they asked me if they could donate some money for her to learn.

On the last day of the trip as we checked out of the hotel, we gave her some money to pay for swim lessons for a week. It was a cool family experience to all chip in toward her gift. All the kids contributed a little, and my wife and I made up the rest. She actually broke down to tears and gave me a huge hug. She was so excited! Her overflowing gratitude put our own good fortune in perspective, and I think those moments will stick in our kids' memories forever. When you see a need, find a solution, and give in the moment, you get to share an experience with the gift's recipient. Over time, kids look for more opportunities to help others, rather than waiting to be told what to do. Reminder: it does NOT have to be expensive to teach your kids to be generous. It doesn't even have to cost money at all.

On a recent trip to Puerto Rico, we woke the kids up at 6 a.m. on the second morning and went to join a beach cleanup group that was picking up trash along one of the beaches. We also worked to filter the sand for plastics and looked for ways to preserve the nature there. Were they exhausted? Yes. Did they grumble at first? Yes. Was it worth it? Absolutely YES. The kids appreciated it once it was done and talked about what they learned in the process.

June 2021, San Juan, Puerto Rico

Please forgive me for sharing so many personal experiences in this chapter. The point in sharing these stories is not to pat ourselves on the back; it is to give you ideas and inspiration for ways to engage your own children. We are not perfect parents by any means and our kids have a lot to learn. But for Amber and me, teaching our kids to be generous and going out of our way to serve feels like we're making a positive impact on our family legacy. We know developing a giving heart will help our kids be more responsible with their money. They'll have experiences that build character and will forge more meaningful relationships over time because they've learned to prioritize giving from a young age.

> "When we go on vacations, we plan some kind of service experience as part of our trips. To prepare one time on a trip to South America, we had our kids choose toys to give away to those in need. It was very difficult for them to decide what to part with. However, while on the trip, once our children gifted their toys away, they were so disappointed to have chosen so few toys to bring. They wished they could've packed suitcases full of toys to bring down to these grateful and humble kids. It was a total mindset shift."
>
> —JARED AND RUTH SINE

BLESSING BAGS

In the past, my family has made "blessing bags" for homeless people. The kids went to Walmart themselves and contributed their own money toward personal hygiene supplies, umbrellas, socks, snacks, and other essential items and filled up a large grocery bag. They got to experience taking cash out of their pocket and picking items off the shelves. Then, with many other friends in our local community, we assembled the "kits" in extra-large Ziploc bags. In the weeks following this, we'd drive around town as a family looking for people who seemed to be in need, and we'd give them a bag. We'd talk about how good it feels to give to people who really needed these items and how we need to be grateful for everything we have.

Making our blessing bags with our family and friends in the community.

Getting them directly involved in the process makes a bigger impression on kids than simply sending money off to an organization, which is why I emphasize pairing donations with hands-on service. Writing a check isn't bad, but these experiences help them see the direct impact of their generosity. They can say, "Hey, I feel good doing things like this. I'm a giver."

It's hard to know what people need when they're on the street or what they'll do with money if you give it to them, which is why I love to help them buy food when they say they're hungry. We always offer to get them a meal and some groceries. Often, they're excited. You can't guarantee everything you give goes to good use, but we'll be judged for our actions, and they'll be judged for theirs. There's a well-known scripture that says you can't judge the beggar and say his situation is his own fault, because when we look to God for help, we're all beggars in our own way.

HOW DO YOU TEACH YOUR KIDS ABOUT HOW TO START A GIVING PRACTICE?

To encourage your child to give money to worthy causes, start with the foundational principles of this book: what is money, and what is it for? Discuss that not all the money we earn and receive is ours to keep. Some of it is to give back and to help other causes. We don't just work to make money and hoard it all for ourselves.

Then, find out what your child cares about. Rather than imposing your own priorities, give them some autonomy. Which causes are important to them? It's easy to go online and help your child research charities that address different issues they care about. You can make it into a research project: similar to using Zillow to learn the cost of real estate, they can use online resources to understand what donation dollars support. If they don't already have a clear idea of their favorite charity, you can give them a list of ten causes and associated organizations, and they can choose the one they're most drawn to.

> *"To whom much is given, much will be required."*
>
> (LUKE 12:48)

Friends of mine give their kids the option of getting a bunch of presents from their family and friends or instead getting one special present from Mom and Dad and making their birthday party into a fundraiser. The kids each get to pick the charity that everyone donates twenty dollars to. One of them always chooses clean water for children in another country. From a young age, they've learned to support causes they care about.

I bring my kids to charity fundraisers such as walk-a-thons. I tell them they each need to bring ten dollars of their own money to donate. Then, we'll walk together and go out to eat afterward to celebrate. They feel much more connected and invested to the cause when they experience a portion of their personal money going to charity than they would if I simply handed them ten dollars to pass along.

"What you have and don't have seems to be relative to your perspective. If you live in an affluent community, it can be easy for kids to start feeling very entitled and lose sight of gratitude for what you have. Some of our happiest times have also been some of the times where we had the smallest budgets. Money does not equate to happiness. It is simply a tool that can buy some freedoms, luxuries, and provide you the happiness of helping others. At the age of three, my children are able to decide whether they would like to receive gifts at their birthday party or have Mom and Dad give them something special and instead do a fundraiser for their birthday party. They have all tried both options; however, more often than not, they have opted for a fundraiser. The one they are most passionate about is raising money to provide clean water for kids who live in areas without access to any.

"I love seeing all their friends donate to the water jug at the party instead of placing presents for them to open (that will likely be broken the next month). We then match their raised amount, and they are able to see the difference of where their money went. Their father and I have also done quite a few humanitarian trips to developing countries where we were able to help put in clean water facilities for villages and were able to show our kids the difference that makes to the lives of children—where something as basic as drinking water is a life-or-death concern. We are trying more and more to facilitate service projects into our vacations as well, and I think this results in a lot less of the vacation whining when there's a touch of perspective added to their trip."

—MELYNA HARRISON, CEO & FOUNDER AT EO PRO LLC

WHAT GOES AROUND COMES AROUND: #SAVETHEKIDS

A good friend of mine named Colin founded a charity called #SaveTheKids. Before he tragically passed away in 2020, we did a series of school speaking engagements, talking about kids' mental health, social media addiction, and other issues.

My friend's death was particularly terrible because he'd been speaking to more than 1 million kids a year across the country—and literally saving kids' lives every day. I witnessed the power of his work myself. After our speaking engagements at school assemblies, he received *hundreds* of messages from kids saying they'd been bullied and contemplated suicide, but they felt better after hearing from us. They decided to delete their social media and uncovered their motivation to be their true selves.

Then, we had a fundraiser event at my house, where he read some of those messages. They brought him to tears. My kids were so inspired by the event. Even my middle son, who was nine at the time, was listening in the background. At the end, he went to his room and came back with a five-dollar bill, which he gave to the speaker as a donation to the foundation.

My friend lived his life with a true spirit of generosity. He'd speak at three schools a day and make such an impact that it would change the whole school. Principals called me three months later saying their entire culture and atmosphere had transformed. He'd planned to fly to Georgia and Florida the week he died, but then he was gone in an instant.

People and supporters around the country organized a GoFundMe for his family. In the first month, 49,000 different people donated a total of over $300,000. He was that impactful because he was such a giver.

In short, I believe you can tell the most about a person by how much they give, not by how much money they make. I raise my kids by this belief, and I believe it's a foundational value that helps good kids grow up to be good adults.

DO TRY THIS AT HOME: FAMILY ACTIVITIES

Get Them Involved. As a family, pick a number of service activities to donate to. Resist the urge to make all the decisions and just drag your kids along for the ride. It's critical to allow your kids to speak up about what matters to them as you decide where to donate. When they have a say, they care more—and also learn empathy.

Go Beyond the Dollar. While donating is certainly helpful, there is nothing that can beat hands-on help. Teach your kids that you can give money, but you can also give something perhaps even more valuable: your time. Find a place to volunteer each year or each quarter as a family using resources like Justserve.org, VolunteerMatch.org, Idealist.org, and Handsonnetwork.org.

Use Talents. We can all give with our time, our money, and our talents. Help your kids focus on that last one. Do they play the piano well? Maybe they can visit a senior center to play music for residents. Is your teen a skilled athlete or artist? Perhaps they can share those gifts by coaching or teaching at an after-school program for disadvantaged youth. Encourage them to think outside the box and to use what they are naturally good at to serve and strengthen others in need.

This is Not a Drill. While many activities in this book have been simulations and dry runs, so to speak, this chapter cannot be taught in theory. Your kids need to give money they personally earn—not money you hand them from your wallet—in order to understand what it means to give. They need to use their own hands to do work and help others to truly understand what it means to serve.

CONCLUSION

Let's cut to the chase: regardless of your income level, I trust you want to raise your kids the right way. You don't want to raise a spoiled child; you want your children to be grateful and financially responsible. You want them to be successful and happy. Right? That's certainly what I want for my kids. And though they have many advantages compared to when I was a kid, they're becoming good people because we intentionally teach them to have a healthy relationship with money.

You have that same power in your hands. Remember what I said in the introduction to this book: this is your moment to shape the financial futures of your kids—and their kids and their kids, likely, because this change is multigenerational. In short, what you do today can prepare future generations to be smart, not spoiled. And, as you've seen with the activities I've included, it can be fun! It starts with you! And it starts today!

For more ideas and resources, visit PacificCapital.com/SmartNotSpoiled.

ABOUT THE AUTHOR

CHAD WILLARDSON, CFF, CRPC®, AWMA®, is the President of Pacific Capital, a fiduciary wealth advisory firm he founded in 2011 that serves entrepreneurs and families. His bestselling first book, *Stress Free Money*, has been featured in *Forbes's* "21 Books To Read In 2021" and on NBC News and Yahoo Finance. In addition to serving the family office clients of Pacific Capital, Chad also manages the $375 million investment portfolio as the elected City Treasurer in his community. Chad is recognized as one of the top wealth management experts in the country and has appeared in the *Wall Street Journal, Forbes, Inc., U.S. News & World Report, Investment News, Entrepreneur, Financial Advisor Magazine*, and two bestselling books: *Who Not How* and *The Gap and the Gain* by Dan Sullivan, Dr. Benjamin Hardy, and Tucker Max. He earned his bachelor's degree in economics from Brigham Young University in Provo, Utah. Chad created and trademarked The Financial Life Inspection®, a unique process to remove the stress people feel about their money.

Chad is passionate about financial education and believes that with the right tools and resources, people can be empowered to make smart money decisions. As a Certified Financial Fiduciary®, he loves to help people organize their financial life, clarify their goals, and make decisions that lead them to a successful and fulfilling life. As a father of five, teaching children to be smart and not spoiled is especially important to him. Outside of his business, Chad loves to travel with his family and enjoys playing and watching sports. Chad and his family are very engaged in serving their community. Besides serving as an elected official, he and his family seek out ways to give back to various charitable causes. Chad served as a volunteer for two years on a church service mission in Lithuania, Latvia, Estonia, and Belarus and can speak, read, and write fluently in Lithuanian. Above all, Chad cherishes his family. A native of Orange County, California, Chad and his wife of twenty years live in Southern California with their five beautiful children.